Pillars of Self-Actualization

Life, The Answer

E. R. LEYVA

Self-Mastery Publishing.

contact@selfmasterypublishing.org.

First paperback edition June 2022

Edited by The Bookshelf Ltd.

ISBN: 979-8-9857946-0-1 (pbk)
ISBN: 979-8-9857946-1-8 (ebook)

Contents

Epigraph

They moved with confidence toward their destination.

They walked their talk in the right direction.

Sometimes slower, other times fast paced,

but always fulfilled through the challenges faced.

Masters of themselves, wisest in their domain,

it was clear to all; they were virtuous, not vain.

Nothing too distracting to divert their gaze.

No ocean wet enough to end their blaze.

With one more step at the end of each day,

they broke through ranks and paved the way.

As time brought wrinkles, and shapes turned blurry,

they gained perfect clarity, that life is a journey.

Preface

Society and those around us are constantly pressuring us into following locally accepted norms—what we should be doing, what we should consider important, what we should believe, and how we should behave. The pressure is everywhere—TV, social media, friends, colleagues, family, adverts, government, you name it.

Today's information overload often makes us uncertain as to whether we are "doing OK" at the game of life or are truly happy with the lives we are living. We often feel unsatisfied with ourselves in a way that is difficult to put into words, let alone admit in public. The Pillars of Self-Actualization series dives into questions and concepts that most of us don't typically talk about because of their sensitive nature. It aims to provide practical answers to some of life's most elusive notions, ones that we constantly struggle to fully grasp.

From the time I became conscious that there was a world outside of my own wants and needs, I have been an insatiable observer of life and human behavior, spending thousands of hours paying attention to my own bias, and consciously looking at different situations from multiple perspectives, always searching for the practical truths behind them—the *real* reasons behind the way people behave and the things they do.

I have recorded these observations in the form of personal notes and unpublished articles for 15 years. During this time, I have identified a series of powerful, often simple concepts that tend to hide in plain sight. When exposed, these notions become an inexhaustible source of practical wisdom that gives you answers when you need them. They make you feel in your bones that you truly understand this life that is filled with events, possessions, emotions, relationships, challenges, failures, and successes, without taking any answer for granted.

The power of these concepts is that they apply to everyone, regardless of their current circumstances. Whether you are looking to become your better self, improve your financial situation, get "unstuck", discover truth, happiness, or the intrinsic long-lasting motivation to finally turn your dreams into reality, I am talking to you. These principles apply to you, and nobody can dictate you the terms for using them. You set the rules, and you judge for yourself.

Furthermore, these universal principles are constantly at work whether you want them to be or not. If you are aware of them, you can use them to your advantage and improve your life, forever. If you aren't aware, then you can't use them effectively. It is that simple.

My commitment to you is that I have not pursued a certain word count to satisfy some arbitrary literary criteria, so you will not find the typical "fluff" found in other self-improvement books. We will not go over the "10 totally unrealistic steps to the perfect life," and I will not ask you to memorize a barrage of fancy acronyms that we both know you will never remember.

My duty is to bring actionable and practical knowledge to the table; knowledge that will build upon your basic understanding of life.

I'm not here to cuddle you with a motivational speech either. I'm here to strengthen the foundation of your thoughts and what you consider important by challenging your beliefs. I want this experience to serve you for the rest of your life, and I hope that if it feels true enough and important enough, you will pass it on, either in your own words or by sharing this book.

Life, The Answer, is the first of the Pillars of Self-Actualization series; short books that expose practical truths which are at the same time, the tools you need to see yourself as you really are. In this first book, we start with some of the most foundational, important, and elusive questions most people struggle with: what is a human life, what is life about, how can I live my best life, and how can I know without question if I am living a fulfilling life, regardless of anyone else's opinion.

"We can easily forgive a child who is afraid of the dark; the real tragedy of life is when men are afraid of light." (Plato)

Introduction

Throughout history, countless people have attempted to explain life. These explorations have generated an extensive range of answers that are often long, cryptic, insufficient, or over-complicated. After hearing them, we are typically left feeling that nothing has really been answered.

Do you have a handy, usable definition of what a human life is? A definition that you regularly use to guide your own life and share with others at times of need? Most people fall into one of three categories:

1. You have an abstract idea of what life is about but find it difficult to put into words. Due to the density of the question, most people settle on popular ideas like life being about happiness, success, purpose, a struggle, and more.

2. You have thought long and hard about it and have a good personal definition of what life is about that you can articulate. If you are in this category, you will know it because your self-made definition is a critical part of your daily life, values, and decisions you make. It brings you strength and empowers you to see beyond the more popular definitions.

15

3. You are totally convinced of what life is about, but you have never bothered to question your definition. Regardless of how you got to your conclusion, you believe your perspective is the correct one and those who don't agree with you are wrong.

If you asked a group of biologists, "what is a human life?" their answers would be fairly consistent and lean toward what is required to create life. You will hear about cells, water, oxygen, and other fascinating, seemingly miraculous processes that create life. If you ask a group of philosophers the same question however, you will get drastically different answers. They will talk more about the purpose of life, what it means to be alive, and why we are alive.

Want to give it a shot before moving forward? Once you are done reading this introduction, try to define what a human life is. If that sounds weird, you can try to define what life is about.

Notice that I didn't ask what the *meaning* of life is. That's a different question that will lead you into a different thought process. To attempt to provide a more robust, personal answer to what the meaning of life is, you should first have an understanding of what life is about. You need a life first because otherwise, there is nothing to give meaning to.

If you rise to the challenge, you may feel like the question is too general, and it may send your mind into a "catch-all" spin: Is it happiness? Actions? Family? Feelings? Success? Nature? A process? What about animals? What about space, minerals, and so on? How do you reconcile all your ideas to give an answer to what a human life is?

"Life" is such a broad topic that people can go in limitless directions when trying to explain and rationalize it. This is why most answers to big questions tend to turn cryptic. People aren't trying to make you miserable with their long-winded answers; there's just a lot to consider.

The easiest way to answer our question is to choose a perspective (say, the biologist's) and provide the answer from there. This is how most people first try to explain anything: they provide their perspective. This method is useful when trying to understand life from a specific point of view, but when we are trying to understand what life is about for any human being, its limits quickly become apparent.

No matter how many different answers we hear to the "what is life about" question, we are almost always left with a bland taste. Something is missing; the answers don't really apply to our own circumstances, or they feel incomplete. Then we settle for the ones that seem kind of right.

What we want is a more universal definition, one that is raw, undisputable, and applies to everyone. It needs to convey what our lives are really about so that we can use it to live better lives. This definition is especially important during times of uncertainty or turmoil; when we need it the most.

Such a definition should be general enough for everyone to relate to but also specific enough to show what makes your life a life. You can only use it to your own benefit if it is clear in your mind.

A proper understanding of what makes your life a life gives you more clarity into who you really are and what is important to you. It allows you to see more easily the direction in which you want to steer your life; it gives you confidence in your decision-making abilities and helps you to better understand the world and everyone around you.

What if we could remove the clutter and define what life is about in a way that makes sense and that anyone can relate to including you? Would you find it useful? Do you think it's even possible?

These are questions that I contemplated for a long time and thought could not have universal answers—until my friend Sergio invited me for a coffee that is.

Sergio is an astronaut who had just returned from a space expedition. Among other things, he wanted to talk to me about some insights he and his crewmates came across while at the Space Station. He took extensive notes of his dialogues and even started recording audio when he realized they were on to something. After we met, he granted me permission to put those insights together into this book.

In part one, I reconstruct Sergio's conversations using his notes and recordings to give you the closest experience possible of how their ideas developed and how they uncovered some very powerful insights. This part is split into four main themes: The Human Perspective, The Path to Fulfillment, Behavioral Profiles, and Application Benefits. The end of each topic is a good place to take a break and think about the concepts discussed.

In Part Two, I share my own notes, which include reflective questions and practical guidance that can help you internalize and utilize the book's insights in your life.

"If you would be a real seeker after truth, it is necessary that at least once in your life you doubt, as far as possible, all things."
(René Descartes)

Ж

Part One: Exploration

The Human Perspective

Arrival

The dialogue that follows is narrated by Sergio. During his first mission to the Space Station, he had a series of conversations with his colleagues that changed the way he looks at life.

"On the day of departure, we were confident and prepared. No matter how ready you are though, a day like this keeps you on your toes with a constant mix of sweaty palms and determination in your heart.

"Luckily, Daisy was there too. We were the only ones going up on that rocket, and I can't imagine a better partner. We've had each other's backs since training camp, to the point where we can often finish each other's sentences.

"Once sat in our rocket with all preparations completed, we heard the countdown: 10, 9, 8, 7, 6, 5, 4, 3, 2, 1… and up we went. We felt the incredible pull of gravity as our rocket accelerated through the sky and into space.

"A few hours passed as we went through the different propulsion stages and made our progress toward the Space

Station. During that time, we mostly monitored different metrics on the dashboards and kept in touch with the team on the ground, answering any questions they asked.

"The trip was fairly smooth; I was even able to take a short nap. When we finally docked at the Space Station, we were warmly greeted by the team who had already been stationed there for a year: my old friend Etienne; Andre, and Tamira.

"Hugs and congratulations behind, we were taken to our quarters to settle in. Our rooms were very small, probably better described as sleeping pods, just a little bigger than a single bed and barely high enough to sit up straight. From there, the team offered to take us to their favorite room aboard. Tamira mentioned it had the best view of Earth in the world.

"As we walked in, we were immediately mesmerized by the beauty of our planet. We appreciated it for a few minutes as we chatted and voiced our amazement. But then, we turned silent as we took it in. In reality, there were no words to describe the view; there is nothing like it.

"Looking at our planet from far away gave me a new perspective, one I had never felt before. It felt as if I was no longer constrained by my personal experience of living here; I could see it for the planet that it really is. It's hard to describe.

"Imagine you were able to float above yourself and see all the things you do and how you live, but unobstructed by your own thoughts and beliefs of being the one on the ground, doing the things you do. You would see yourself from a detached perspective where your actions no longer feel personal, they become mere observations. That's how it felt.

"The room we were in was what we would consider small in size, and everything was attached to the walls so that nothing could float away. The concepts of ceilings, walls, and floors are less important there since you can literally stand upside down all day long if you want, but it seems like we naturally preferred to stand straight in comparison to each other, at least for the time being; it made the space less chaotic.

"By the window was some equipment that looked like an oversized telescope. The crew said we could zoom in enough to see people moving on Earth!

"After some time, our minds started shifting from admiration, becoming more analytical of what we were seeing. That's when our conversation kicked off."

"Wisdom begins in wonder." (Socrates)

What Is Life?

"To think that this planet holds everything we know about life," said Etienne with an inquiring voice.

Daisy looked at him playfully and replied, "Except for the people in this room of course."

"Indeed," Etienne whispered as he gazed at the long distance between us and Earth, "except for us fools out here."

"Do I detect some nostalgia there?" I asked playfully. "Is a year on board taking its toll on you?"

"Well, I am a social being after all; I miss my family and my friends. But rest assured, I still appreciate this incredible view."

"Not only is all of life there," Daisy added, "But everyone's lives are different. Over seven billion people are thinking and doing different things all the time."

"Right on!" I said as I calibrated the telescope to take a closer look. "We can see parts of Europe, Africa, and Asia now!"

Tamira helped me with the controls, "You should look for the pyramids of Giza," she said.

I zoomed in, located Egypt, and moved toward the east to find the River Nile. I then moved north to find the cities of Giza and Cairo next to each other. The pyramids sat just west of Giza, right where the desert began. "I see them. They look absolutely gorgeous! I can see groups of tourists visiting, and there is the Sphinx too! I definitely have to go there one day."

"Glad you like it! I was there once. The scenery is truly magnificent, and I look at it from up here sometimes."

"One day!" I confirmed.

"All right, let's see the beaches of Mykonos!" Sure enough, there were tourists relaxing by the water and cruise ships at the port. It looked like a great vacation day over there.

I started feeling like I was taking too much time from everyone, so I said, "Okay, okay, one more. Paris..." and there it was, with plenty of people walking around the Eiffel Tower.

"Ooh, *la France*. I do miss an evening walk through its small streets full of restaurants, the outdoor seating, ordering a *raclette*, and enjoying the atmosphere as it gets dark."

The room turned quiet again, so I looked up and moved away from the telescope. Etienne was deep in thought, so I asked sarcastically, "What's going on? Did I bore you already?"

"On the contrary, your narration of what you're seeing is actually making me think about life. Is it just about different people going around doing different things?"

"That's certainly what I saw through the telescope a moment ago, but I'm sure there's more to it than that."

"You're right," Tamira agreed. "People do more than just move around. We need to account for much more... Why are they doing different things? What makes the difference between one

27

person's life and another? Could one person's life be better or more correct than another's?"

Daisy answered as if she'd anticipated the question, "I don't know about better or more correct, but people are born in different places, to different parents, and in different cultures. They then experience different things as they grow up and live. The events they go through definitely make a difference in their lives. For example, your country of birth and where you grow up will define who you interact with simply through geography and language. These interactions contribute to who you become and shape the way you look at things."

"That's certainly true, Daisy," I replied. "I think we can relate to the events you speak of as all of the experiences people go through in their lives. They're what we would typically call our 'past', or our 'life story'. Everybody's life story is different, and these differences unquestionably impact the things we do.

"Following your line of thought, as these events and experiences happen in people's lives, they must have thoughts and feelings about them. What they think and feel must also make a difference. For example, one person may be happy that you offer them a free chocolate bar, while another one may think you are trying to mess with their diet and will become uncomfortable with your offer. Same event, two different thoughts and emotions."

"For the record, I'll eat that chocolate bar any time," interrupted Etienne.

"Noted, Etienne!" Daisy replied with a smile.

"So, Sergio, I think you are saying that even if two people are from the same place, speak the same language, and have the same culture, the same event can still mean different things to them. Is that right?"

"That's right. Another example that comes to mind is in sports. When your team wins you are happy, when your opponent's team wins, not so much. Same event again, different thoughts and emotions."

"Thanks, that's a much better example that I'm sure we've all seen many times! So... the things we experience in life create a sort of baseline that impact the things we later do, but just as importantly, the thoughts and emotions we have about these experiences further differentiate our actions from each other?"

"You got it."

"Then," Daisy continued, "As people live through events and have thoughts and feelings, they end up making decisions and taking actions. Building on the chocolate example, the person on a diet could decide to not eat that free chocolate bar because they're trying to lose weight. They could then act by accepting it and putting it away, or by politely declining it."

"Makes sense," I replied. "It seems as if people's lives are a chain of events, a process in which we experience something, have thoughts and feelings about it, and then make decisions and take actions accordingly."

She partially agreed, "Seems right. However, I think we should keep in mind that the chain of events from experiences to actions is not always simple to trace. For example, if you

29

experienced the event of seeing someone fall and quickly took the action of helping them get back up, the link is very easy to understand. They fell; you saw it, felt bad for them, thought you could help them, decided to help them, and helped them, everything happening very quickly.

"On the other hand, if you experienced more tragic events in the past, such as being betrayed by someone you love, you could become more suspicious of others in the future for a period of time, or even for life. If at some later time you became suspicious of someone, it could be for a mixture of reasons, one of which could be your experience of betrayal from a long time ago."

"Great point Daisy; I can't disagree. Your example shows how both simple and complex experiences are driven by the same process, even when the links are far apart."

"That's it!" exclaimed an excited Tamira, coming out of her thoughts and attracting everyone's attention. "Actions are really all you can see through the telescope. We don't see any of the other parts of the process because they are not visible to the eye!

"Think about it, people's lives are different because they live through different events, have different thoughts and feelings, make different decisions, and take different actions. But all we are able to see are their actions. The other pieces are hidden in their minds; no one can see them. Those really seem to be all the things that make our lives different from anyone else's."

"I like it, but are we sure it's really *all* the things?" Etienne asked, unsure. "What about plants, animals, food, and water?

Shouldn't they somehow be part of what makes our lives too?"

Andre, who had been quiet but listening attentively stepped in. "Sure, there are plants and animals. We also breathe, eat, drink, and sleep. However, including them is beyond the point of understanding life for our everyday use. To go any further down that path, would be to try to understand life in the context of how all external things impact us. Can you imagine trying to list how every single thing impacts a person? There wouldn't be enough days in a lifetime. To my mind, if we are looking for what makes *people* different, it doesn't make a difference between you and me that we both eat and drink, or that Earth has plants and animals."

"I think I see where you are going, but please expand on it."

"When we talk about life, we usually talk about what life is about for us as humans. You've heard and used the old cliché, 'that's life'?"

"Sure, many times."

"Well, people tend to say this when they want to highlight that something which happens all the time has happened specifically to them.

"For example, you get a flat tire and so miss an important appointment. You tell your friend, and they say, 'Yeah, something like that happened to me too. It sucks, but that's life.'

"Or you get lucky and win some on the lottery. If you don't want to show off too much, you might say, 'I just got lucky this time; that's life, you never know when it will happen.'

"But what do you think we actually mean when we say, 'that's life?' I don't think it's related to anything else beyond what life is about for us humans. I think that defining what life is about for a human is much simpler and more practical than defining the entire spectrum of life for all living organisms."

"I think I agree with your logic," Etienne replied. "But I feel like we're not all on the same page about what we are exploring here. My initial question was about *all* of life, not just about humans."

"You did say, and I quote, 'Is life just about different people, just going around doing different things,' did you not?"

"I did indeed," Etienne conceded.

"I think you would agree then, that even though you may have been thinking about all of life to some degree, your question was primarily about people—humans. You didn't ask what it takes to keep all these people alive; your question was more philosophical."

"You're right. I guess my focus was really on understanding what life is about for people. My apologies."

"None needed my friend; dialogue is the way of progress."

Etienne nodded in appreciation.

"It is the mark of an educated mind to be able to entertain a thought without accepting it." (Anonymous)

The Human Life

I picked up the baton. "If life is such a large topic with so many ramifications, could we simplify it by saying that a human life is the equivalent of what one additional human life adds when added to, or subtracts when removed from the concept of life in general?"

"Interesting thought," mused Etienne. "Tell me if I've understood you correctly. You are proposing that within all things that make life, or the totality of life—plants, molecules, animals, age, purpose, meaning, and a million other things—if we can single out the things that are added when a baby is born or removed when a person dies, we could consider those things to define a human life, within the boundaries that Andre just mentioned."

"That's what I propose, yes. But now that I hear it back from you, I agree we need to include Andre's boundaries in it. It would be what a human life adds or removes from life in general from the perspective of a human. For example, from the perspective of a dog, an additional human life could just be the addition of guaranteed food, shelter, and play time—"

"And love!" Daisy shouted indignantly.

"Yes! And love," I smiled. "But in all seriousness, we don't know if plants or other animals think about life, and if they did, how deeply could they think about it? Within our human intellectual capabilities and limitations, we must consider that

33

only humans can think about life in any depth—at least until we find alien life that we can communicate with. Until then, we are trapped in our human minds and our human bodies."

"One question on perspective," Andre said. "When you say, 'from the perspective of a human,' do you mean from the perspective of any human (i.e. there are infinite perspectives), from an agreement between humans, or from humans other than yourself?"

"An important question indeed," I answered. "Tell me if this makes sense. If the perspective of a given person was that human life is about hurting other people, I wouldn't have much appreciation for that person's definition. It wouldn't be good enough to apply to every human being. The definition of a human life should apply to *every* person. It should be provable and true to the best of human knowledge, and therefore, unquestionable or extremely difficult to disprove, and as you pointed out earlier, practical."

"That's a difficult balance to attain."

"Quite right. Whatever definition we can come up with here would be sure to face criticism and disagreement—there are close to eight billion people after all! Nevertheless, disagreement doesn't automatically make the definition wrong—the entire world could argue that two plus two is not equal to four and be wrong. By the same token, some people still genuinely believe Earth is flat, yet here we are looking at a sphere.

"If there is not enough substance to logically explain a conclusion, or if the best existing conclusion can be called into

34

question, or if competing conclusions are easily disproved by logic and facts, then disagreement is futile and pointless.

"On the other hand, if constructive discussion, such as the one we are having, or newly discovered facts lead to a better definition of a human life than the one we come up with, then the better definition should take its rightful place at the top."

"That makes sense," Andre agreed. "I think we are onto something good here. We are saying that a human life is equal to what a human life adds to life in general from the most accurate perspective humans can produce. Earlier, we said that people go through life experiences, have thoughts and feelings, make decisions, and take actions. Are these the things that a human life adds to life in general?"

"You read my mind!" shouted Tamira, becoming very animated again. "That means that I am who I am, or my life is what it is today, because of the events I've experienced, the thoughts I've had, the feelings I've felt, the decisions I've made, and the actions I've taken. I can certainly agree with that! All our lives are different because of these things, while at the same time, they are also what my human life adds to life in general. Really brilliant! I did those things in my past; I do them in my present, and I'm pretty sure I will do them in the future, unless something tragic happens to me, knock on wood. I can see how life is these things!"

Daisy looked thoughtful, "I'm not sure I'm fully there yet. I think I get it, but I don't see it as clearly as you seem to. Have we really arrived at a proper and complete definition of what a human life is?"

"If you still have doubts, then it seems not," said Etienne. "What is it that doesn't connect for you?"

"Well, I don't see my life as just being defined in terms of experiences, thoughts, emotions, decisions, and actions. I think I also bring good energy to those around me; I care for others, and I care for the environment too. Our definition feels a little limited as it stands."

"Thank you for bringing forward those concerns; it's good to know I'm not alone," Etienne replied half-jokingly. "I wasn't able to express myself as well as you just did, but that's in line with what I was feeling earlier when Andre schooled me.

"Here is how I am coming to see it based on our discussion so far. Let me ask you a few questions and tell me if it improves our definition."

"Sure, let's try."

"When you mention that you care for the environment and that you bring good energy, how is it that you come to do those things?"

"In terms of bringing good energy, I try to be understanding of others and focus on positive and good things. In caring for others and the environment, I'm always willing to help those around me; I give time and money to causes that are good for the environment and am careful to limit my own polluting."

"Great. Then, would you agree that focusing on positive things, understanding others, taking care of them, and being environmentally conscious are results of your thoughts, emotions, decisions, and actions?"

"Interesting way to put it. I have to say yes; there wouldn't be any other way."

"At the same time, could we say that Sergio's friend, the one who wants to hurt everyone, also arrived at his conclusion of what life is about through the same method?"

Daisy chuckled, "I suppose so, yes, through thoughts and feelings about his likely negative experiences."

"Wouldn't that mean then that adding you to life brings the things that you spoke of to life, and adding Sergio's friend to life adds the things he spoke of to life? And adding both of you to life added two people with the capacity to live experiences, think, have emotions, make decisions, and take actions, regardless of what those became?"

"That makes sense, and by removing us from life, you would remove the same. It's starting to click; please keep going."

"Oh, that's as far as my wits go," he joked. Everyone laughed.

I joined back in. "Thanks for the examples, Etienne. Let me try to create one last visual scenario to see if we can bring this home." I looked around the room for inspiration, spotted a metal box sticking out of a wall, and flew over to it.

While pointing at the box with an open palm, I began my example. "Imagine this box is a small robot. Right now, you see a box, but just replace it in your mind with a small robot that is about one foot tall and has a head, arms, and legs, just like a human being.

"Now, let's say the people in this room are very smart. Let's say we can program this robot to do anything we want at all, no limits."

"We are literally rocket scientists!"

"Yes, yes, Etienne, but it will take more than rocket science to program this robot."

"Bring it on then!"

"As I was saying, we are going to program it to start living today and to die 100 years from now. This way, the robot will have a pretty long life by human standards.

"We are also going to give it a hard drive so that it can store information with a near-infinite capacity. This hard drive will function extremely fast, as fast as our brains, and it will also be able to make connections between different pieces of information, just like we can."

"Please, expand on those connections," Etienne replied.

"Sure thing. Think of something that is white on the outside and yellow on the inside. What would you come up with?"

"An egg, of course."

"There you have it: that kind of connection. I never had to mention eggs for you to take two colors and the concept of inside and outside and make the connection that this is probably an egg."

"Perfectly clear. Please carry on."

"Very well. We will program the robot to be able to think freely and experience emotions, just like a human. To finish off, we will program it to make its own decisions and take action on whatever it wants.

"We now have our robot and will release it into the world today with the capabilities we have programmed into it.

"Throughout its lifetime, this robot will learn things, think, feel, decide, and take actions at will because that's just what it does. We could have programmed it to just roam around the house picking up trash, but we didn't. This robot does more things, and those things it does are what the robot's life adds to life in general. That is what the robot's life is about..." I paused for a second to allow everyone time to digest.

"The robot cannot have thoughts and emotions if it has no information stored in its hard drive. It cannot make decisions and take action if it has no thought or emotion. It will keep doing those things until it dies aged 100. The robot's life is to do those things we programmed it to do, continuously, for its entire life. It is a connected and integrated process where all the features we programmed are needed for the process to work correctly. Are you still with me?"

"I'm with you," Daisy replied. "You mean that regardless of the consequences of the actions of the robot, or of the things that happen to the robot during its 100 years of life, what the robot adds to life in general is that it can store information, think, feel, make decisions, and take actions. Remove the robot and you remove those things it added to life."

"Great, looks like we are on the same page. Now, replace the robot in your mind with yourself. Those are also the things that you do day in, day out. You have no way around it. You can't stop it, and you couldn't change it even if you wanted to. That is your life today and will be your life every single day until your last.

"Think about it: you can't stop experiencing things. Even if you decided to sleep an entire 24 hours to skip a day and prove us wrong. You will have lived through the experience of sleeping 24 hours.

"You can't stop your brain from thinking. Even if you decided to meditate for 24 hours, meditation doesn't stop your thinking; it simply unclutters it.

"You can't stop yourself from feeling. Even if you repress your feelings, or if you're going though a depression where you say you feel nothing inside. That itself is a feeling, a feeling of emptiness.

"You can't stop yourself from making decisions. Even if you say you're not going to make a decision for 24 hours. That itself is a decision that you would uphold for the entire day.

"And finally, you can't stop yourself from taking actions. Even not taking action is an action."

"I can see it now," concluded Daisy making robot-like movements. "I'm a robot."

"Well, great talk," Andre replied. "This has definitely given me a lot to think about, and I don't want to stop our conversation so abruptly, but we do have things to do in this spaceship. Shall we resume later?"

"You bet!" Daisy replied. Everyone else confirmed.

"Great. Sergio, I imagine this conversation can be used in your assignment to evaluate our mental health while you are here?" he asked.

"You are sharp, Andre, and correct," I replied.

"Then we need to make the best of it... Everyone, please take a few minutes to organize your ideas or take notes on what we just discussed so that we can continue later," Andre instructed.

"Once you are done, let's shift gears and meet at the command station in 15 minutes to get our new visitors up to speed on what we have been up to."

Over the next three hours, we received an intensive refresher in the do's and don'ts of the different areas of the ship, listened to updates on the experiments taking place at the time, and then went to bed.

"By three methods we may learn wisdom: first, by reflection, which is noblest; second, by imitation, which is easiest; and third, by experience, which is the bitterest." (Confucius)

41

The Fruit and the Tree

Nine hours later, we were all gathered for our first breakfast in space—which is nothing to be jealous of—and getting ready to begin our workday.

Daisy casually returned to yesterday's conversation, "I couldn't stop thinking last night about what a human life is. I started using our definition in combination with happiness. I was thinking that if a human life is about living experiences, having thoughts and emotions, making decisions, and taking actions, then we should be able to work out what a happy human life is about."

"Do tell," Etienne lifted his gaze, making eye contact.

"I have often thought that life is about accumulating happy experiences. However, if our definition is correct, a happy life would not just be about the accumulation of happy experiences, but also about being at peace with our own response to any experience. By responding to a negative experience in a way that makes us feel good, we can find some happiness where there wasn't any. This is why we can't anchor our happiness to any number of experiences or material things, because life is much wider than that."

"You remind me of that quote that's attributed to Buddha but that no one really knows the origin of," Tamara replied. "Peace comes from within. Do not seek it without."

"Exactly."

"That all makes a lot of sense, and I'm not saying it's wrong," Andre interjected, "but I have hardly ever seen life that way. To me, life is about goals, about achieving lifelong objectives. I feel like to accept this definition, I would have to accept that my thoughts about what my life is about have been wrong all along, and I certainly don't feel that way."

"You do realize we haven't even had coffee yet, right?" I remarked, seeing how deep the conversation was getting. "But I like your question. This is where our definition of life starts to contrast with today's pop culture. Many people today see life as the pursuit of a set of goals. They see happiness or success as the achievement of those goals, or as Daisy mentioned, the accumulation of happy experiences.

"Don't get me wrong, it's good to have goals and to move in their direction, and it's good to have happy experiences, but goals are simply not enough to be life. Goals fit within the human life; the human life does not fit within goals. Hear me out...

"The human life is about waking up every day knowing and embracing that events will happen, that you will think and feel things, and that you will make decisions and take actions. That's it. No more, no less. Every human gets the same gifts. What you do with them is your business. With these same gifts, some people with unlimited amounts of money in their bank accounts are unhappy most days, and some people with very little money are happy most days."

"I agree with all of that too," Andre replied. "But it doesn't change the way it feels in my mind—that my life is about goals.

I need to be able to reconcile this contradiction if I am to accept this definition of life. I feel like you are asking me to replace something that I know is central to my life with something that I can't yet fully relate to."

"Fair enough. Thank you for that insight. Just to be clear, I'm not trying to replace your beliefs. Let me ask you a few questions to see if we can reconcile our definition with your goals."

"Go ahead."

"There are many versions of what people consider life to be about. For you, it's goals, but for someone else, it's about happiness; for others, it's about purpose, or family, and so on. Do you think any of them is wrong?"

"I don't."

"But if life is about goals, then the person who thinks that life is about purpose must be wrong, no?"

"I can't impose my view of life over what anyone else's view of life may be. If purpose is as real for them as goals are for me, then it just means we have different ways of looking at life."

"I see. Then could we say that people can only arrive at their conclusions of what life is about through their life experiences, thoughts, feelings, decisions, and actions?"

"Sure, I'll give you that. I know what life is about for myself because I can think about it."

"Then I have one more analogy for you. Could we say that these different conclusions are like different flavors that people prefer, similar to different fruits that grow in trees? They don't necessarily dislike all the other fruits; they just prefer a specific fruit."

"Got it. I prefer the fruit of goals, and you prefer the fruit of happiness."

"Great. And what would you need to get your fruit?"

"A tree, I guess."

"I'm glad you said that, but you could have also said money so that you can buy your fruits. Why didn't you say that instead?"

"Because I was thinking of what is required for the fruit to exist at all, not just how to get it."

"I see. So... if you wanted juicier and better fruits, you would agree that it's important to pay attention to the tree, not just the fruit?"

"Definitely."

"And would this be true for everyone, regardless of their preferred fruit?"

"It would be."

"So if you didn't pay much attention to the tree, you may still have some fruit, but you would never know how good that fruit could really be, unless you took care of that tree the best way you could."

"Sounds about right."

45

"By the same token, if we arrived at the conclusion that goals are 'it' for you, or that happiness is 'it' for me through this process of experiences, thoughts, emotions, decisions, and actions, wouldn't it be important to pay attention to those in the same way that we would pay attention to the tree to get better fruits? Would it not allow you to get better goals and allow me to get better happiness?"

"Interesting. So, I'm the tree in your analogy. I don't have to let go of my goals as central to my life. You are saying that I produce my fruits no matter what, but that understanding the definition of a human life is like understanding how to take care of myself, the tree. It would lead me to produce better fruits, so better goals."

"Indeed I am, Andre, but there is more. You may be the tree in the analogy, but the tree only produces fruits. You, the human being, produce much more than just fruits. You don't only produce goals. You produce the perspective of your life, your habits, your behaviors, your personality, your relationships, and everything else you think of. Being conscious of what you use to produce these things will help you improve their quality."

"Gotcha. So you mean that by understanding this mechanism that is universal to all people, I would consciously pay attention to my thoughts and emotions during the events that I go through in my life. In doing so, I would make decisions and take actions that are better aligned with the things I consider important.

"This does seem right. I'm thinking that even though the pursuit of goals is central to my life, it's not about the number

46

of goals I am after, but about achieving goals that I consider important. Anything that helps me define more important or more fulfilling goals is a plus in my book, and the tree analogy really hit the spot. I must take care of the tree for better fruits.

"By accepting that life is about the events I live through, the thoughts I have, the emotions I feel, the decisions I make, and the actions I take, I am not diminishing the importance of goals in my life, I actually understand that goals are simply a fruit of my existence. My existence means that I live, think, feel, and do things. I no longer feel like I have to choose one or the other; I can see how one supports the other."

"Impressive reconciliation and conclusion, Andre. You even combined decisions and actions into doing things," remarked Etienne.

"I second that compliment," Tamira added. "But I do have to make substantial progress in one of my experiments today or I'm going to hear it from Ground. Can we continue this later?"

"We must."

"There are three classes of people: those who see, those who see
when they are shown, and those who do not see."
(Leonardo Da Vinci)

The Path to Fulfillment

The Life Video Library

A couple of busy days went by without much talk about the subject. But then, three days later, we were lucky to not run into any issues and finished our maintenance, labs, and tests earlier than expected. It felt like we'd finished early for the weekend, and we all welcomed a break.

We gathered at our favorite room, and the topic returned. Once again, it was Etienne who casually introduced it, "You know guys, the last few days have been a little different for me. I feel like I have more clarity over what my life really is about and like I'm living more in the present."

"Funny you should mention that," Daisy replied. "I have been feeling the same way. I've been playing back different parts of my life and have found comfort in revisiting my thoughts. I've taken a look at some things I've been through that have bothered me for a long time and found that considering the situation, I responded in the best way I could at the time to most of those events.

"I think internalizing our definition of a human life is helping me to get closure on a few experiences and to realize some of the things that I could have done better. I feel a sort of relief from the past and from material things that I can't quite explain."

"It seems we stumbled upon a very important concept but have not fully defined how to use it," Etienne concurred.

"I like where you are both heading there," I said. "I have actually been thinking about just that over the last few days too. I have an idea of how we can identify its value and how to use it—if you are up for diving into it? What do you think?"

"Let's do it!" he replied. "But can we recap where we left off if you don't mind?"

Everyone else in the room seemed up for it too. I grabbed my notepad, "Great idea. Let's take a look at the notes I took at the end of our last conversation.

What is a human life?

- To the best of our knowledge, the most practical and accurate way of defining what a human life is involves identifying what adding one more human being to life adds to life in general from the perspective of a human.

- Through discussion, we arrived at the conclusion that every human we add to life has five key capabilities through which we create an infinite number of life journeys. These capabilities make for a complete and practical definition of what a human life is. They are:

1. The events we live through and store memories of in our minds. These experiences can be in or out of our control.

2. The thoughts we have about the things that happen to us, around us, and that we become aware of.

3. The emotions we feel about these same things.

4. The decisions we make that impact ourselves and others.

5. The actions we take that lead us in certain directions and also impact ourselves and others.

- We are destined to do these things during our entire lives whether we want to or not. In fact, we are incapable of not doing them.

- Everything we humans do is through these five integrated capabilities.

Did I leave out anything?"

"Sounds about right to me," Andre said.

"Great. Now, picture having access to a library of everyone's lives. It would be like a super high-tech video library where you could see the events that happened, the thoughts and feelings anyone had at any given moment, the decisions they made, and the actions they took. Imagine you could rewind, pause, play, or fast forward to analyze any piece of it at any time."

"That is some library…"

"Indeed, Tamira, what an incredible technology it would be, full of videos of people from all walks of life; from the happiest to the unhappiest, and every stage in-between.

"Then imagine if we could use this information to find the most important factors that lead people to feeling fulfilled and so live a fulfilling life. Wouldn't that be useful?"

"Sure it would," replied a doubtful Etienne, "but such a library could obviously never exist…"

"Great observation!" I answered somewhat sarcastically. "But I will go out on a limb here and say that we may achieve a similar level of insight if we just imagine that we have it."

Andre chuckled. "That seems like a long shot, but we have some time. I'm willing to dive in as long as this doesn't turn into a totally irrational discussion. You're supposed to make sure our mental health is OK, Sergio, not make us go crazy."

I laughed.

"I'm in too," Tamira and Daisy answered simultaneously.

"Let's proceed then!"

"Before we start," Andre interrupted. "Do define what you mean by fulfilling please, so that we're all on the same page."

"Good point. I think it's easier to define fulfilling by first thinking about satisfaction. When you are satisfied with something, it means you are at peace with whatever it is you have, whatever happened, or whatever will happen. It's the minimum threshold of what makes you feel content.

"If the result of some situation is below your satisfaction threshold, then you are not satisfied with it, and you will have thoughts and feelings in accordance with the unsatisfactory result. It's your reaction to the outcome of a situation or your anticipation of the outcome.

"Fulfillment is quite deeper than satisfaction. It's not simply about crossing a threshold of what you are willing to accept; it's also related to your feelings about yourself. For example, if you were part of a team that carried you to first place in a competition where you didn't help at all, you may feel satisfied with the result because you won, but not fulfilled because you know you didn't contribute."

Tamira rephrased the concept, "That's interesting. So fulfillment is not only being at peace with the events that happen in my life, like winning the competition, but also with my thoughts, feelings, decisions, and actions related to each of those events."

"You got it."

"What about happiness though?" Daisy asked. "I feel like it's somehow tied to fulfillment. Are you using fulfillment as a synonym of happiness or do you find a distinction between them?"

"Great question. I see a slight but important distinction between the two, even though they are very close terms as you suggest.

"Happiness can be caused by different things. For example, the excitement of your upcoming birthday can create some happiness within you. When you hear good news about someone you love, you could become happy because you care about them. These moments of happiness don't necessarily mean you are fulfilled, yet you are happy. I am defining fulfillment as in the peace within you that makes you feel good about yourself and also leads to happiness, but in this case, it's a more stable, long-lasting source of happiness."

"I see; that makes sense. So, by finding the most important factors that lead people to live fulfilling lives, we're also finding some of the most important factors for living *happier* lives," Daisy said.

"Wonderful," I continued. "If there are no other objections, then let's begin our exploration in search of the recipe to the fulfilled life!

"If you look to others for fulfillment, you will never be truly fulfilled."
(Lao Tzu)

Directionally Correct

"We can start by looking at Earth through our favorite window. We see a planet with land and water, continents, many countries, and even more cities. The planet has many people living on it and other living organisms such as other animals, plants, insects, bacteria, and so on. There are many more details about this planet, like the atmosphere, minerals, and gravity, but we won't enumerate them all today. I think we get the picture; we are looking at Earth.

"If we used our telescope to zoom in to a large city, we would see several buildings, streets, and highways. We would also see many people in this city. If we had our high-tech video library, we would essentially be able to pick one person in any city, follow them from birth to death, and know every single thing about them—their experiences, thoughts, emotions, decisions, and actions, at all times."

"That would be a lot of information," Tamira exclaimed.

"It would be indeed. So let's try to keep things simple, or at least start with a simple example."

"Fair enough," she agreed.

"Imagine we picked our person. Her name is Jane, and she is a manager at a local company. Her workplace is about 30 minutes away from home if she takes the fastest route. We know however, that there are hundreds of streets in this city and tens of thousands of intersections. This means that there are millions of possible routes to go from home to work.

"Most of these possible routes are completely unproductive, such as those that go in the opposite direction to her destination. Some routes are more efficient than others; some have better scenery than others; some are free to use; some involve paying a toll; some are safer than others, and some are simply more familiar to Jane. The better she knows her city, the easier it is for her to pick the best route based on how she wants her trip to work to be.

"When it comes to Jane going to work, we don't really need a high-tech video to know if she is headed in the right direction; we just need a map of the city and her trajectory. Whether Jane picked her favorite route or the fastest one doesn't matter; both routes would be directionally correct."

"Unless," Tamira interjected, "her favorite route involves going two hours in the opposite direction, two hours back, and then the 30 minutes to work."

"That's right, four-and-a-half hours for a 30-minute route is a little too much for directionally correct... Nothing crazy so far I trust, Andre?"

"Nothing crazy."

"Let's become much more ambitious then. What if we wanted to apply the same concept of tracing a trajectory on a map from point A to point B, but not simply for Jane's physical movements? What if we wanted to trace the trajectory of all the other things that make up her life? We would want to know if Jane's life is moving in the right direction."

"Wow, how can we claim to know what the 'right direction' is for anyone?" Tamira asked, sounding somewhat defensive.

"Glad you asked. If a certain way of life would make Jane feel fulfilled, being on the trajectory of that certain way of life would be the right direction, and—"

"And," Tamira interjected, "since we know everything about Jane because we have her life video, we know what would make Jane feel fulfilled."

"Precisely."

Etienne stepped in with an uncomfortable look on his face. "I'm not sure I agree. What if Jane gets laid off tomorrow and needs a job to feel fulfilled? Would that mean that she's going in the wrong direction until she gets a new job?"

"Good question, Etienne," I replied. "Let's think about it. If Jane was laid off, which part of her life would be impacted?"

"What do you mean? Her professional life, or her ability to sustain herself, I guess?"

"That's probably correct, but I apologize. I think I asked the wrong question. I meant, according to what we defined life to be, which of the five categories does getting laid off fall into?"

"Ah! Well umm.... It would be an event in her life?" Etienne answered with shaky confidence.

"Right, and what would that trigger?"

"Thoughts and emotions," he said.

"Right again. And what would those thoughts and emotions trigger?"

"Decisions and actions."

"There you have it," I replied. "So, armed with our knowledge of Jane's life video, in this case, we would know that her career is very important to her. If Jane decided she was going to spare three hours a week to think about her next step, would you say that she would be going in the right direction?"

Etienne smiled and straightened his posture, "I would say she is going in the right direction for three hours a week."

"That's a valid perspective. So by that, you must also mean that she is far from being on the highway to solving her situation."

"Right, she is driving through many streets and in multiple directions that don't take her any closer to her destination. She's only driving toward that for three hours per week."

"I like how you used a map there to visualize Jane's situation, but before we talk any further about maps, I think we need to clarify one thing due to the nature of our example.

"Would we agree that if Jane needed some time to herself so that she could 'disconnect' before figuring out her next step, that 'disconnection time' would not be considered idle time? It would be a conscious decision made by Jane because she felt that it would allow her to collect her thoughts and properly decide her next step, regardless of what that step would be. In this scenario, we would say that Jane is moving in the right direction—as long as her disconnection time was not an excuse to avoid dealing with the situation."

"Agreed," he replied. "The fact that Jane lost her job doesn't mean that she is now going in the wrong direction. It's just an event that happened in her life that she has to deal with. As long as she is doing the things that will take her toward feeling fulfilled, she is moving in the right direction, and there are different speeds at which she can get there."

"Perfect. So far, we've used Jane's life video to understand if she is responding appropriately, or in accordance with her own desires, to a negative situation that happened to her. In this same way, we could look at any event that happened to Jane, whether positive or negative. We would see if she reacted in a way that is consistent with her truest values and beliefs at any time during her life.

"As long as her response is consistent, she is moving in the correct direction or is directionally correct, regardless of her speed.

"Now, before it escapes us and if there are no objections, let's see if we can use the map Etienne hinted at a minute ago.

"I can't change the direction of the wind, but I can adjust my sails to always reach my destination." (Jimmy Dean)

59

The Life Map

"Let's say we had a map that was very similar to the map of a city, only it was of Jane's life. It would accurately show not only her physical movements but also her thoughts, emotions, values, needs, wants, desires—everything related to her. It would also contain all the possible trajectories that she could take, and we could see if she were moving in the right direction at any time."

Andre, who wasn't looking convinced, chimed in. "Wouldn't it be possible for Jane herself to be confused about what her correct direction is in life, and for it to be clear to us who are looking from the outside with a technology that doesn't exist?"

"That's quite accurate, Andre. If everyone was perfectly clear about their map, they would follow the perfect path toward wherever they wanted to go, making the perfect decisions and taking the perfect actions every time. But I think you would agree that few people are ever close to perfectly clear."

"I somewhat agree, but please continue your point."

"The difficulty for us humans is that it is very easy to think that life is success, career, money, or how many material things we have; we get lost in the fog of so many options and lose track of what's really important inside of us. Material things are nice, and there is nothing wrong with wanting and having them, but they do not define a human life.

"Our lives are an experience, unique to each of us. Living a fulfilled life should be independent of our material possessions or what may be qualified as success by others. It's important that when we mark destination goals on our map, we don't set the incorrect ones."

"Let's be real though," Andre interrupted, "you can't tell me that material possessions are not important."

"To be sure, I am definitely not saying that. I don't want to discount the comfort and positive emotions that material possessions can bring in any way. Those things are important. What I am trying to convey is that you don't actually need those things to live a fulfilled life. Allow me to play you a quick scenario and tell me if we agree."

"Let's hear it."

"Picture two people. One with an expensive, luxurious car, and one with an inexpensive, but just as reliable car. Does having the expensive car make that person more fulfilled than the person with the less expensive car?"

"Not necessarily, but they could be."

"Fair, but as you said, not necessarily... The material possession, which is the car in this case, is not a factor in whether the person feels fulfilled or not. It can indeed be fun and comfy to have a luxurious car, but that's as far as it goes once the 'new purchase novelty' expires. Feeling fulfilled goes a little further. It's about how you feel within yourself regardless of what you have.

"The only thing that counts toward how you feel within yourself regardless of any material possession is the quality of your thoughts, emotions, decisions, and actions. And the best part about it is that you get to decide what quality means for you."

"Okay, I see it. If I considered it quality to have negative thoughts and feelings, to wish harm to people, and to hurt people every chance I get, then I would be a fulfilled, evil person."

"That's quite drastic, but yes. The material possession doesn't matter. Our definition of life doesn't pick what is good or evil. All it does is to expose the core of how we function as human beings, which in turn allows us to use it as an intuitive compass to navigate life and set the right directions in our map."

"Makes sense, I can see what you meant now," Andre conceded.

"Perfect. Going back to Jane: if she understood what life is about, then in the scenario where she lost her job, the burden on her emotions would be much lighter because even though a negative situation had happened, she could find comfort in the realization that she is responding in a way that makes her feel fulfilled. She would feel good about her thoughts, emotions, decisions and actions. It would eliminate the confusion you spoke of."

"I see," Andre replied. "So, Jane would be confused if she made a rushed decision or took action without allocating time to properly digest her emotions and think about the situation. If she did this, she would risk moving in the incorrect direction on her map.

"On the other hand, if she internalized our definition of a human life before running into this situation, it would allow her to react in a way that would more likely aim her in the correct direction regardless of her speed, and at least help her to feel the satisfaction of properly dealing with the situation."

Daisy stepped in with a non-negotiable tone. "I think we need to make another clarification here. If Jane really needed money for survival—for rent or some other emergency—and she jumped at the first job she found, even if that job was contrary to her deepest goals, values, and desires, this should not be considered in the opposite direction to her fulfillment."

"That's a tough one, Daisy; but I appreciate the clarification," I replied. "In the same way that decisions and actions that are taken quickly because of an immediate crisis are not necessarily wrong decisions that would take you in an incorrect direction, we cannot arbitrarily call them right decisions either.

"In this case, the most important thing for Jane would to be conscious of what she is doing.

"Her path, like everyone else's, will have obstacles that will sometimes require taking a step back or an unexpected detour. Remember, fulfillment is not about winning all the time or having everything go perfect. As you mentioned earlier, fulfillment is about being at peace with your thoughts, emotions, decisions, and actions during both positive and negative events."

"I can agree with that. I just wanted to make sure that we're not painting someone as rash just because they have to survive," Daisy accepted.

"Point taken; I think we are all in agreement. But you did make another very important inference there that is worth noticing.

"The way you reacted to Jane's story is very important as it shows true empathy for her situation. While some people may try to project their own life map onto others by arbitrarily deciding if Jane's actions are right or wrong, you immediately understood that Jane's life map is unique and different from yours, or to put it another way, that what applies to you doesn't necessarily apply to her. This makes you a tremendous listener!"

"Thanks," she replied awkwardly, "but I'm not sure I understood what you just said."

"I think I do," Etienne chimed in. "I'm thinking of a friend who is fond of giving life advice to everyone around her. She is extremely smart and very successful by most people's standards, but with time I came to realize that the advice she gives is based purely on what she considers important and to be right for *her*. She pays little or no attention to what the other person considers important. This ultimately makes her advice almost useless to the person receiving it because she is skipping over that person's values, desires, and goals. I think this is what Sergio means when he says some people try to project their map onto others."

"That's exactly it, Etienne," I replied. "Thanks for the much clearer example."

"I see it now." Daisy returned. "If we had the video library and the life map, then to truly understand whether Jane was moving in the correct direction through any situation in her life, we would need to leave our biases aside and look at each situation purely from her perspective of what she ultimately considers important. Only then would we be able to offer her meaningful life advice."

"I wish my good friend would realize this," Etienne replied thoughtfully.

"Life must be understood backward. But it must be lived forward."
(Søren Kierkegaard)

Changing Direction

"This is super deep guys," Tamira observed. "If there was a map of Jane's life, it would somehow include everything that would make Jane feel fulfilled. But we are human beings, and human beings change. Jane's desires are likely to change with time, aren't they? If her desires change, wouldn't the map change too?"

I laughed. "I can see this panel won't give me an easy pass! That is a fair point indeed. Let's explore it.

"The first thing that comes to mind is that change implies switching from one direction to another. For example, if Jane is driving her car on the way to a friend's house, and suddenly her friend calls to tell her that it would be better if they met at a coffee shop instead, Jane would change direction to the coffee shop.

"The impact on her trajectory depends on how far she has already traveled toward her friend's house and how far the coffee shop is from where she is right now. The same would be true for the map of life—"

"Meaning that," Tamira interjected, "if you studied eight years of medicine toward becoming a surgeon and decided to change to engineering, the change would be larger than if you decided to switch to some other medical profession like anesthesiology."

"That's a good example too. The impact on your trajectory depends on what you changed to and how far it is from the path you were on before."

"That seems clear enough," Daisy nodded.

"Now, so far we've only traded one thing for another. But in reality, the map of Jane's life doesn't only have one desire in it. It has hundreds, even thousands.

"For example, if Jane's current vision of her near future is of a good job, a husband, a house, and two kids, but then she goes through heartbreak and decides that she would actually prefer to be alone for a while, the impact on her trajectory is not as clear as it is in the career or coffee shop examples we've just discussed. Her breakup doesn't have to impact her good job, so her direction in that regard could be intact, but it may very well impact her plan for a house and kids.

"Her circumstances have changed, and this has affected her vision of the future. What's important to see here is that fulfillment is not about making all of Jane's visions of the future come true. That would be impossible, and probably reckless. It's about Jane being at peace with herself in the way she reacts to any situation. This tells us that the map of Jane's life is much more complex than the two-dimensional map of a city we are used to. Jane's map seems to have more dimensions to it because it includes more things.

"What's more, we probably can't even imagine exactly what such a multidimensional map would look like. But rest assured, we don't need to imagine unimaginable things. We can certainly imagine a regular two-dimensional map and know that the life map is similar but provides much more information in some way that would make sense to us if we had it."

"Got it," added Andre. "So, in Jane's life map, there is a location for every possible destination she could go during her life, whether she goes that way or not. At the same time, when something like her relationship situation changes, it's as if she's on a highway and was initially planning to take exit 15, but there was some road issue and now the next best exit for her is 17. Her direction is still the right one even though something changed."

"Great analogy, I love it," Tamira smiled.

"So far so good then," I replied. "Now that we see how Jane can pick a different direction to move to, and also how changes in her life don't necessarily mean that she changes her overall direction, we can answer Tamira's question by making the point that Jane's map itself doesn't actually change. Jane's understanding of herself changes, and this is what gives the initial impression that the map will change, but actually, it is her direction that changes within the same map. People are always learning new things and are therefore always updating their understanding of themselves and the world.

"In her life map, Jane is always on the road, even when she sleeps. She doesn't just move on the map of life when she needs to go from point A to point B; she is in life 100% of the time. She is alive and she is going somewhere at all times. The better she understands herself and the world, the more consistent her actions will be with what fulfills her, and the fewer drastic changes she will need to make. The less understanding she has, the more likely she will need to make 'knee-jerk' adjustments throughout her life."

"Can you talk a little more about what you mean by being in life 100% of the time and those knee-jerk adjustments based on understanding myself and the world?" Daisy asked.

"Sure can. We all have some vision of what we want our lives to be like. It's blurrier for some than for others, but we all have it. It could be as simple as wanting to be happy, or to be surrounded by people, or to accomplish some goal, or to be a certain kind of person, or to play a certain sport, and so on. The more thought you've put into it, the clearer and stronger this vision is and the less likely you will need to drastically change it.

"If we go back to Jane's breakup for example, she could have realized that she actually doesn't want to have kids, or that she actually likes women and can finally break free of an invisible oppression she has felt for a long time. She could also see it as a relationship that didn't work and know within herself that her vision hasn't changed; she could still want the same things, just with a different person. The better Jane knows and accepts herself and the world she lives in, the less dramatic adjustments she will need to make to stay on track with what fulfils her."

"The only thing that is constant is change."
(Heraclitus)

69

Multiple Directions

Etienne looked as if he were still processing this last piece of information, so I paused. He noticed that I was reading him.

"You caught me playing through another scenario in my mind," he smiled. "Help me through this. What if I thought that the way to happiness and fulfillment was money and so spent years of my life running after it without much care for anything else? Then, having acquired the fortune I wanted, I realized that money was good but that I also wanted other things: a close family, friends, etc. How would you describe that situation with regard to the map of life?"

"I think that's another great example. Let's visualize it." I fetched my work clipboard, flipped it to a blank page, and created this graphic as I talked through it.

Image 1

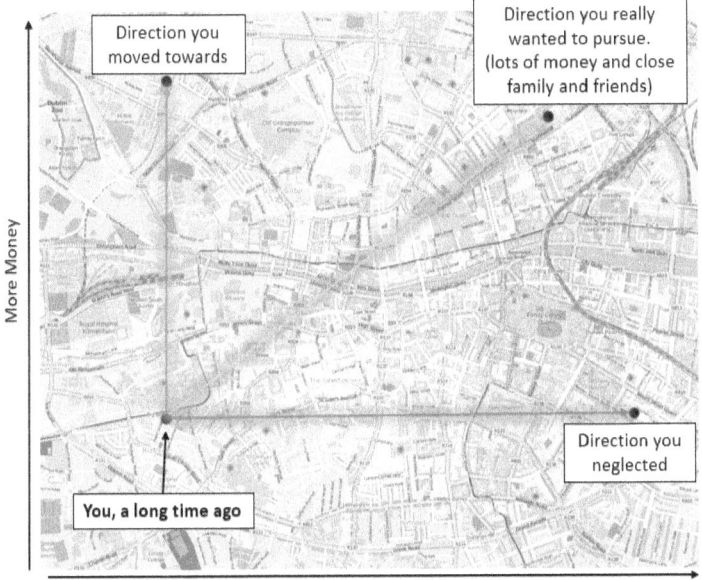

"In this chart, one direction takes us toward more money, another one other takes us to closer family and friends, and a third direction takes us to both.

"In your case, we would see on your life map that you moved only in the direction of money, not in the direction of other things important to you.

"When you finally opened your eyes, you realized that you had reached the money destination you set for yourself, but not the other one.

"Unfortunately, there is no magic wand that can just change that. This kind of experience happens to all of us in one way or another. We do things that we can't take back or just fix. If it's not too late, you could start moving in the directions of

71

those other things that you consider important and make the best of it. If it's too late, then let that be a valuable lesson and still try to make the best of it through your thoughts, emotions, decisions, and actions." I made an alteration to the chart to demonstrate this:

Image 2

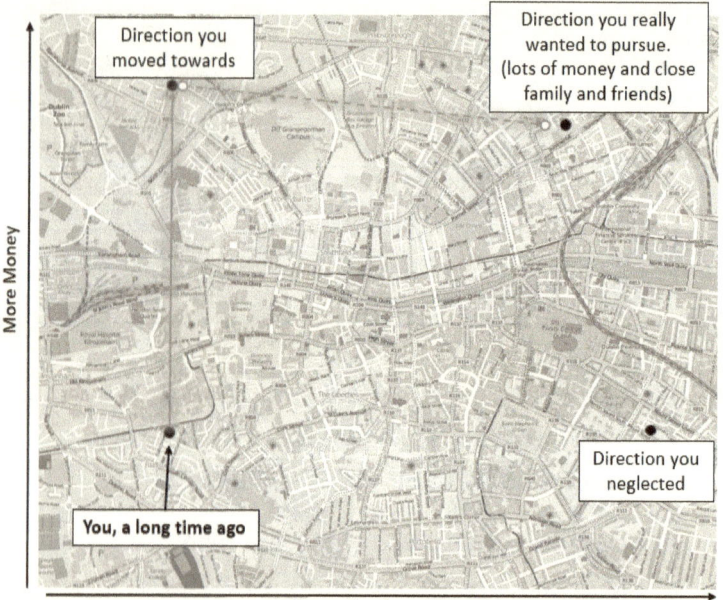

"As I mentioned earlier, the better your understanding of yourself and the world, the fewer drastic changes you will need. Would you agree that 'less understanding' can lead to 'more incorrect understanding' if one is not careful?"

"I do."

"Then that was the problem in your money example, and it is extremely common throughout society. You thought you knew what was important, but you didn't have a correct understanding of what your life was really about. This lack of knowledge caused you to take your life in a direction that was insufficient to bring you long-term fulfillment. It's the compounding effect of ignorance.

"When people become aware that they have followed an incorrect or incomplete path, in many cases, the emotion is so hard to deal with that they close themselves off from it, digging themselves into an even deeper hole, causing all sorts of irreconcilable negative feelings.

"It takes courage to look at oneself, see our imperfections, and accept that we make mistakes. Without doing so, we remain a prisoner inside our bubble, unable to start moving in the better direction because we refuse to accept that we have made mistakes."

"Sounds like a bummer."

"Sadly, it is. On the bright side however, it's important to note that although in this money scenario we're examining, you may have understood the issue a little too late, not all circumstances need to be so sad. If you realize on the way toward money that you also want closer friends and family, you can incorporate those elements in your route before it's too late. That way, you improve your route and keep going, without any major upheavals."

"Fair enough, that makes sense. We have progressed quite a bit. Can we summarize where we've got to before my head explodes?"

"Good idea. We believe we have accurately defined what a human life is from the perspective of a human: events, thoughts, feelings, decisions, and actions.

"We then questioned whether this information is useful at all, and I claimed that it would help people live more fulfilling lives.

"After that, we created the concept of a 'life video library', which contains videos of everybody's life, and we can access and analyze those videos at will.

"This led to a concept of a 'map of life' that we can use to see if someone's life is going in the right direction according to their own life characteristics. Did I miss anything?"

"Well," Andre suggested, "all these concepts of high-tech libraries and multi-dimensional maps you created are supposed to let us extract, to use your words, 'the most important factors that lead to people feeling fulfilled and living a fulfilling life.' But to be honest, all I see so far is science fiction."

"Ah, I think I'm starting to trigger Andre's crazy-meter. But I'm not ready to quit yet—unless you think that our thought process so far is flawed and that if we had the library and the map, we would still not be able to find those most important factors to fulfillment? I thought we were in agreement a minute ago?"

"With the video library, and the map, *and* enough time, I think we could figure it out," Andre replied. "But I hope you are not about to come up with some other unimaginable artifact."

"The worst of all deceptions is self-deception." (Plato)

74

Knowing Your Direction

"No promises, Andre, but let's carry on! If we were able to play Jane's life video, which we can rewind and fast-forward at will, on top of her map of life, would we expect to see that Jane has always gone in the right direction?"

"Certainly not!" Daisy replied instinctively. "No one can always travel in completely the right direction in every area of their life. People make good and bad decisions all the time."

"I must agree with you. So, we should expect Jane to not always have gone in the direction that would make her feel fulfilled but also to have gone in all kinds of directions, sometimes in perfect alignment with her objectives, other times, not so much."

"Definitely."

"Well then, since we agreed earlier that Jane has many needs, then sometimes, and in some areas, she will be aware of where she is going—she could be moving in the direction of an objective she wants to accomplish, and/or living by a specific set of values. Other times, she would be less aware of where she is heading and start going in circles or living part of her life on autopilot."

Etienne, always thoughtful, observed, "I can think of a lot of people going in circles and on autopilot back on Earth."

"Me too," confirmed Tamira.

"Glad you agree," I replied. "Then, the next question should be pretty obvious to you: Would you think these patterns of behavior are particular to Jane, or are they common in most people?"

"Common to everyone, surely."

"Thank you. As we keep moving forward, though, we should start to see that everyone is following some kind of path at all times. This path will inevitably become clear once they have followed it long enough, even if they weren't aware that they'd started along it."

"Will it? Can't we look back and not know why we did certain things?"

"Indeed, we can. It is often difficult for people to recognize the path that they are on, and it takes courage to see the reality of one's missteps. If a person is neither able to see nor recognize the path they have been following, that doesn't mean the path doesn't exist. That person has been doing things for days, weeks, months, even years that have led them to where they are—it's those things that expose the path they have taken.

"But to answer your question, we have to be realistic and practical with this concept. It doesn't matter what flavor ice cream you ate one summer day four years ago or why you decided to gamble that extra $5 three days ago at the casino. Single instances of relatively insignificant events don't make or reveal a path. But if you were to tell me that you've bought the same ice cream every single day for the last four years or that you gamble more than you can lose at the casino every week, I wouldn't necessarily need to know *why* you have done those two things for so long to figure out that you may not be on the right path."

Daisy became inspired, "That's right! As people's preferences constantly change and they move along the different routes in their life's journey, it becomes easy to stray from the ideal path that they tend to fantasize about in their own minds.

"At times, their decisions or indecisions must lead them in a different direction from where they really want to go.

"Other times, they would find themselves on a path that they didn't intend to take, one they were pushed onto by external factors or because they didn't see it coming.

"In some cases, they may even follow one route further than they would have liked until they realize and ask, 'what the hell am I doing here?'

"But luckily, if things work out, they find themselves on the right path at the right time and feel kind of awesome."

"I couldn't have said it better," I agreed. "In this journey of falling off the path and coming back to it over and over again, it is practically impossible for a person to be on the right track 100% of the time. Some claim that they are always on point, but that is typically a symptom of their inner blindness.

"Can you imagine if every single aspect of your life was not only on track but also to the extent that you wanted it to be? I can't even begin to imagine what that would look like! Would it mean everything would have to be perfect? The perfect lover, family, friends, and career? And what would perfect even mean? No obstacles? No issues? Or just the right amount of each?"

Andre was tickled. "I don't know about you guys, but I'm always on track. I am that 0.001%!"

"Sure you are," Tamira replied with a roll of her eyes, making everyone laugh.

"If you do not change direction, you may end up where you are heading."
(Lao Tzu)

On and Off Track

"Alright, let's keep going," I said. "Although everything in our lives may not always be 100% on track, the idea of keeping our lives directionally correct—on the right track in most areas, most of the time—is not far-fetched. There are people who really seem to have the map of life figured out. They seem to stay on track far longer than the average person and seem to have the keys to the puzzle we are trying to decipher."

"I can certainly think of a few people in my life who seem to be on track more often than others too," nodded Etienne.

"Me too," Tamira agreed. "I have several role models who have guided their lives amazingly. I think of them often and look up to them in many different ways."

Very humble of you, Tamira," I said. "I have several role models myself from whom I get constant, unlimited wisdom, even when they are not present. It feels kind of magical. I just think of their personalities and the values I learned from them while going through the many events life throws at me, where I don't see an obvious best response. Doing this fills me with strength and reveals a little bit of their wisdom that doesn't necessarily come naturally to me. It helps me make more confident and more informed decisions."

"So, what you are saying is that you often ask yourself, 'What would Andre do?' and get a sudden rush of insights and wisdom?" Andre joked.

I laughed. "How did I know you were going to say that? But yes, something like that." I paused and then began to sum up our discussion. "So, staying on track for the longest amount of time possible is critical to living a fulfilling life; I think we all agree on that. But based on what we have just been discussing, it may not be the most important factor."

Etienne seemed confused. "How so?"

"Well, we know that people change their minds all the time and that each of those changes has the potential to lead them off their desired track. I think the key factor is that some people are much better and faster than others at figuring that out, and either adjusting their destination accordingly or getting back to the right path.

"Let's use Jane and one more person for this example: Brian. Let's say they are fulfilled by exactly the same things and have both been working for the same company for four years. Suddenly, they received the news that they've lost their jobs. We already know that Jane spent a considerable amount of her time figuring out her next best step, whatever that may be. Brian, on the other hand, wasted a month on autopilot, lost confidence, and decided to do something else, even though he was happy in his old job. Wouldn't you say that Jane got back on track much faster than Brian?"

"It depends. This seems overly simplistic. What if the 'something else' that Brian did turned out to be the thing he loved best in the world? We don't always know where a path will take us, and sometimes, we 'fall into' things by mistake, ending up on the right path without knowing such a path even existed. By contrast, Jane had a fixed idea in her mind, thereby limiting the paths she could take and meaning she might miss out on what could have been a far better path."

"Thank you, Etienne, for not letting us move forward with lazy explanations. I must accept I chose my words too precisely and provided a poor description on that last point, so please allow me to rephrase it with your perspective in mind, as I completely agree with what you just said and think you will agree with me too."

"Let's hear it!"

"I was presenting a scenario where two people feel fulfilled by exactly the same things. They both lost their jobs and dealt with it differently.

"I mentioned Jane spent a considerable amount of time figuring out her next best step. I can see how this could be interpreted as having a fixed idea. However, I also said, 'whatever that next step might be,' meaning that Jane didn't limit herself at all; she reached into herself to really find what she wanted to do next, to connect with what makes her feel fulfilled. She could have made a change or followed that dream she'd been putting off, and either would have been just fine.

"I can also see how when I said that Brian 'wasted' a month on autopilot and then went on to something else, it may have sounded as if I was judging Brian, but I wasn't. We agreed earlier that time spent collecting your thoughts is not wasted time. When I said that about Brian, I meant that he literally did waste it, he avoided dealing with the issue; he didn't try to collect his thoughts; he just went onto autopilot.

"You are correct that even on autopilot, he could luckily fall into his ideal path. But I think we would agree that even a broken clock is right twice a day and the purpose of our inquiry is not to base our path on sheer luck, it's about consciously sculpting it to our fulfillment."

"I must agree that we agree," Etienne chuckled.

Our greatest glory is not in never falling, but in rising every time we fall.
(Confucius)

The Master Formula

Daisy had been quiet for some time and seemed lost in thought. Etienne brought her back with a wave of his arm. "Hey there, did we lose you somewhere?"

She blushed. "I was still thinking about Tamira and Sergio's comments about their role models and how they seem to think of them as if they were present even though they're not physically there. A good friend of mine who went through some serious trouble came to mind. I always find strength in remembering her story because she managed to remain relatively happy and energetic through the thick of it. It's as if nothing fazed her too much. Whatever happened, she found a way to adapt and overcome without throwing her life in the garbage.

"It makes me feel as though some people have a consistent and intuitive thought process that allows them to make good decisions most of the time."

"Yes!" Tamira enthused. "That's definitely in line with what I was feeling a minute ago!"

Andre agreed, "Interesting, I relate to what you are saying. In all honesty, I feel that I very rarely make major mistakes, and as you give your examples, some people I know personally who fit those qualities to a tee also come to mind. They don't seem to make mistakes; it's like they have life all figured out. I can't help but get the feeling that all these good qualities are somehow related and often come bundled together as a sort of package of virtues."

"Help me understand here," Etienne interrupted. "Are we saying that there is a possible 'master formula' that could theoretically allow anyone to become successful? Almost like a perfect list of behaviors that would lead to fulfillment if followed? That wouldn't sound very realistic to me."

"Indeed, it wouldn't be, Etienne. Everyone's correct path in life is different, which means that there is an infinite number of correct paths. What makes any person feel fulfilled is the correct path for them. We would need to write a manual for how to behave in all situations and from all perspectives, which is impossible, not to mention terribly inefficient."

"I'm with you, Andre," Daisy said. "Even if we were to say that going to school and college, or even practicing a religion were the most important parts of the master formula, we would only be restricting all the paths that don't follow the agreed norms."

"I agree too," I added. "Even twin sisters who grew up together and essentially received the same education would have different correct paths. For one, it could be to become a professional athlete, while for the other, it could be to become a scientist. The examples are infinite; each person's correct path is based on their life experiences, thoughts, and emotions, not what anyone may try to impose on them.

"I think we are of the same mind in not trying to mandate how people should live their lives. Our exploration is about exposing the principal factors that allow people to take control of their lives, so that they can use them to pave their own way to fulfilment—and by lives, we mean—"

"Yes, yes," Tamira interjected with a robotic voice. "Experiences, thoughts, feelings, decisions, and actions."

This seemed like a good opportunity for a pause, so I offered it. "We have been on topic for a good amount of time now. Should we give it a break here and come back to it later? We will need Andre to tell us about these packages of virtues to continue our investigation."

Andre nodded in approval. "That works. I'm sure we all have some personal catching up to do since we've worked non-stop for the past few days. Etienne, do you want us to summarize again?"

"I got it already. I'm just adding three bullets to the last summary:

- We defined a human life as being experiences, thoughts, emotions, decisions, and actions.

- We claimed we can help people live more fulfilling lives by properly understanding and using this definition.

- We invented a life video library to stalk people like no one has ever stalked anyone before, which is admittedly kind of creepy.

- We invented a map of life that somehow captures every possible path anyone can take in life. We cannot fully visualize this map, but somehow it doesn't matter because we can think of a regular two-dimensional map and believe that it works in a similar way.

- Then, just now, we talked about being directionally correct, changing directions, and of how people fall on and off their path toward fulfillment on their map all the time.

- We all agree that some people appear to be better at staying on and/or getting back on track than others. This seems like an interesting point to explore as it may help us to extract insights that could help people live more fulfilling lives.

- Finally, Andre, will enlighten us all with a majestic explanation about virtues next time we talk."

"Ha, right on, I like it! Have a good evening everyone, whatever that means to you up here!"

"When I was a child, my mother said to me, 'If you become a soldier, you'll be a general. If you become a monk, you'll be the pope.' Instead, I became a painter and wound up as Picasso."
(Picasso)

Behavioral Profiles

Formulating Behavioral Profiles

In what would be considered the next morning on Earth, we came together again for breakfast. I was the last one to arrive, "Good morning everyone."

"Morning, sir. You slept well?" Andre asked.

"Like a baby."

"Great. After the marathon we've had over the last few days, I'd say a good night's sleep was well deserved."

"Sure waaaaaaas," Daisy yawned.

"You'll be glad to hear that today should be pretty relaxed. I checked in with Ground earlier and all our projects are on track. We just need to keep an eye on things, do some routine clean up and maintenance, and enjoy the view."

"Yeeeeeey!" Tamira exclaimed, conjuring some excitement. "Does that mean we get to hear about your package of virtues this morning? I'm intrigued by it."

"Why not? Did Sergio have his coffee yet? We wouldn't want to start too fast or we could lose him."

"Very funny, Andre. We're all ears."

"All right then! Any initial thoughts before we start?" Andre asked.

Etienne had one. "I spent some time thinking about your package of virtues last night as I tried to sleep. Then I began to realize that if such a package of virtues—one that allows people to live more fulfilling lives—really does exist, there must be other traits that are often used to describe people which can also be grouped together."

"Clever!" Andre replied in surprise. "I think you may have nailed it. If we really had Sergio's high-tech library with people from all walks of life, we would find three groups of people, each with a different set of dominant behaviors: one would mostly exhibit virtuous behaviors; the second would mostly dwell in ambiguous behaviors, and the third would mostly struggle with vicious behaviors."

"Interesting," Etienne mused. "My thoughts were more around virtuous behaviors and wrong behaviors, which you seem to call vicious, but I see you've added another set there that you call ambiguous behaviors."

"That does sound a little strange, Andre," Tamira said. "How did you come up with these? When it comes to behaviors, I usually think in terms of right and wrong too."

"Well, let's get to it. The package of virtues I hinted at yesterday is really one of the three behavioral profiles I just mentioned, the virtuous behavioral profile. I think it's best we start our discussion from the ground up so that we can all see what makes a behavioral profile. Then, if you all agree, we can discuss each of them separately."

Everyone nodded.

"Great. Let's build a new behavioral profile from scratch by taking a quick look at honesty versus dishonesty. Do you think any one person could be purely honest or purely dishonest?"

"If by purely you mean 100% honest or dishonest, I would say no," I replied. "Everyone is a mix: sometimes they are honest, and sometimes they're not."

"Great," Andre said. "Then do you think any one person could be exactly half honest and half dishonest?"

"That's a strange question," I said as I searched my thoughts. "When I think of honesty, I usually see people as either mostly honest or mostly dishonest. I've never thought of anyone being exactly half-and-half."

Andre didn't seem surprised. "I actually agree with you. Do you think that a very honest person and a very dishonest person have similar thoughts?"

"I would think that the dishonest person needs to make many calculations regarding what they say and do that the honest person doesn't have to make. Also, the honest person likely has more peace of mind," I said.

"Fair enough," he replied. "Would you agree that someone who is mostly honest is more likely to also be more trustworthy, better intentioned, and a better person overall than a more dishonest person?"

"I would agree to the extent that it's more probable that the honest person also possesses those qualities. In reality, we can't say that every honest person is also, say, a well-intentioned person. You could be honest about your ill intentions too. And to anticipate your next question, I would also agree that the dishonest person is more likely to not be well-intentioned and to just be someone I would prefer not to associate with."

"So you read minds now, huh?" Andre joked.

"Only sometimes," I laughed.

"Alright. If we thought hard and long about it, we would probably manage to identify between five and ten traits that are more common in honest people. With this list, we could then talk about a behavioral profile called 'Honest Behaviors.' We could say that people who display any of the behaviors that are part of this profile are also more likely to display the other behaviors within the same profile. It works as a reinforcement loop where behaviors that share a common essence reinforce each other without us even being conscious of it."

"Makes sense," Etienne pondered. "But you had mentioned three behavioral profiles: Virtuous, Ambiguous, and Vicious. Is this a fourth profile we need to add to our list, or is it something that fits inside of the Virtuous Behaviors?"

"I believe honest behaviors fit within the virtuous behaviors. As you can imagine, we could come up with countless behavioral profiles to analyze anything we want. Further breaking down behaviors into honest or dishonest could be useful, but I think that for the scope of our conversation, which is about living a fulfilled life, the three I initially mentioned are all we need."

"Fair enough," Etienne conceded.

"Great. Now that we see how these behavioral profiles are formed, we can imagine that within all the potential ways we could behave when faced with all the events life throws at us, everyone has a dominant set of behaviors. If we think back to our honesty example, it's not easy for someone to quickly change from being mostly honest to mostly dishonest and vice-versa, it takes time.

"In other words, people's behaviors don't randomly flip between mostly virtuous to mostly vicious or mostly ambiguous. People are consistent in their behaviors, even though they may not notice it, and usually, if they change their dominant behavior, it's through a gradual change over an extended period of time, not through a sudden change.

"Makes sense," Tamira replied. "So, we now know how to form these behavioral profiles. But you mentioned we could make an infinite number of profiles depending on what we wanted to analyze. Why did you pick those three?"

91

"Ah yes, I hadn't answered your initial question yet, Tamira, but we are headed there now. I first thought about comparing three people: the most successful in terms of following the correct path on their map of life, the least successful, and the one who is bang in the middle. I then used those three reference points and matched them to how I would describe all the people I know, were I to place them into those three buckets.

"You are probably thinking this is a huge generalization, and I would agree, but when I boil it down as much as I can, I bucket people into three main categories: people who consistently do stuff right; people who consistently do stuff wrong, and people who are in a gray area where it's not as easy to determine whether they fall into the right or wrong buckets—if you can bucket them at all."

Tamira approved. "A generalization indeed, but it's as good a starting point as any for talking through it, I guess."

"Right. We are aware that in reality, no one can be described by any single set of behaviors. In other words, no single person can be fully described as only exhibiting virtuous behaviors—doing the right things at the right time, being ambiguous all the time, or doing everything wrong all the time. In reality, every person is a mix of these three behavioral profiles to varying degrees, but I think it's important to first look at them separately to help understand their key differentiators.

"Once we understand these, I believe it will become easy to identify the dominant behaviors we choose in our own lives and the dominant behaviors those around us have chosen to adopt."

"Makes sense; let's give it a shot!" I said eagerly.

"Your worth consists in what you are, and not in what you have. What you are will show in what you do." (Thomas Davidson)

The Virtuous Behaviors

Andre began, "The behavioral profile we touched upon yesterday was the virtuous one, which is, as we have been saying, doing the right things at the right time. In this case, our first subject picked from the life video library is Silvia. We can think of her as an extreme example of someone who mostly dwells in virtuous behaviors.

"Looking at her entire life, we see that Silvia was very much attuned to her life map and was on the correct path almost the entire time. We can see in her life video that she made decisions in accordance with what was important to her, by always taking into consideration her short-term and long-term desires.

"As we take a deeper dive into Silvia's life journey, we see that she didn't take any specific road to reach the destinations that fulfilled her in her life map. Sometimes, she was on the highway, other times, she took the streets. She met roadblocks and got a few flat tires along the way, but she was always directionally correct and didn't need to make too many unnecessary U-turns. She did indeed have a small number of 'off-track events', but these didn't last long as she quickly picked herself up and got back on track."

"She sounds quite impressive," Daisy mused.

"Good point," Andre acknowledged. "But to avoid misrepresenting Silvia as some kind of superstar, I think it's important to note that she is not someone we would typically picture as an extraordinary person; she is perfectly, quote-unquote, ordinary. She wasn't gifted with what we would call a genius mind and was never totally financially secure in her lifetime. Additionally, she felt the entire range of emotions we all feel, from happy, to sad, to devastated by loss, to being in love and loved back, and so on. And just like everyone else, her life had ups and downs, with a good share of problems and a few lucky moments.

"What allowed Silvia to live a fulfilling life was how well she knew herself, how well she was able to accept her qualities and flaws without arrogance or shame. How well she was able to realize her mistakes and her accomplishments without either hurting her self-esteem or over-boosting her ego. Silvia lived a happy, fulfilled life."

"Forgive my interruption, Andre," Daisy said, "but how is it that Silvia gets to know herself so well? I can see how knowing oneself better leads to living a more fulfilled life, but how such self-knowledge is achieved is a little puzzling."

"No worries; I was heading there next. In short, you have to be willing to fully accept yourself, while at the same time, not being complacent about yourself. It may sound silly, but it's not easily achieved.

"Here is an example from back before I decided to go to space and was still in business school.

"Say you were a chef, and you opened a restaurant that became very successful. Would you decide to expand and open a chain of multiple restaurants?"

"I probably would," Daisy replied.

"Okay. How many additional restaurants would be enough? Two? Five? Ten? A hundred? A thousand?"

"One hundred restaurants sound like a lot to manage. I'd say five to ten."

"Perfect, but here, Tamira would prefer a thousand restaurants and—"

"I never said—" Tamira started.

"Bear with me. Tamira wants one thousand and Etienne only wants one restaurant because he wants to make sure that he has total control over the quality of his establishment. Are any of you wrong in your decisions?"

"I guess not, at least for as long as we don't change our minds."

"Good point. So it's important not to rush such an important decision in case you change your mind somewhere along the way. At the end of the day, going from one restaurant to five in one swoop is a huge step; you'd probably start with a second restaurant and then build up, right?"

"Right."

"Great. In business, this is part of your personality as an entrepreneur. Everyone has different levels regarding how much they want to control, how comfortable they are delegating responsibilities, and how much they can stomach to risk. A successful and happy person with a single restaurant could quickly become unhappy and unsuccessful with multiple restaurants. At the same time, if Tamira has a single restaurant, she may not feel fulfilled because she wants a thousand."

"I'm with you."

"To know that you are on the right track, you first have to make peace with yourself and gain an understanding that the things that make you feel fulfilled are neither better nor worse than anyone else's; they are just your things. You have to resist the temptation to let life push things on to you or make decisions for you because you're not paying attention. You have to consciously draw your path the way you want it as life unfolds, doing so in a way that is consistent with your beliefs and values.

"If a savvy salesperson talked you into going from one restaurant straight into one thousand, it could be a great business opportunity, and you could certainly go for it. But the first questions to ask would be, 'Is this decision taking me on my path to fulfillment, or am I trading my life dream of overseeing my own ten top-quality restaurants for someone else's dream? Am I about to get locked into licensing and franchising my business? Tamira would be happy and fulfilled with the franchise option, but would you be happy and fulfilled? Imagine Etienne; he would be pulling his hair out!"

"Interesting," she replied. "I can picture what you just described, and it makes perfect sense. I can see what you mean when you say that to live the most fulfilled life possible, I have to know myself, and I need to be able to accept that my preferences are no worse or better than anyone else's. At the same time, I shouldn't allow that acceptance to become a comfort-zone cushion that keeps me from self-improvement and from moving along my path to fulfillment."

"That's right. The danger in accepting yourself is, as you say, becoming complacent. It's important to pay attention and not deceive yourself into thinking that something that gives you a good feeling, such as eating fatty foods, is automatically fulfilling. Many people go down this type of path for years before realizing they need to change."

"Got it. But since you bring up change, what if I thought I wanted my life to be a certain way but later on realized that I want it to be in a completely different way? Would changing my direction mean I haven't been doing the right things and therefore, mean that I'm not virtuous? Would that make me a non-virtuous or vicious person according to your definition of virtuous behaviors?"

"Well, a few thoughts here: Remember we all have a mix of the three behavioral profiles within us, and this mix doesn't just apply to a single part of our life. For example, you could make bad decisions with your career and great decisions with your family. No one is fully right or fully wrong if all the components of their entire life are taken into account.

"Then, everyone has a time in their life when they become aware of things that they were not aware of before. It's normal to course-correct as you become aware of new things about yourself and the world. This, however, is a very different story from dramatically changing your life because you have been suppressing your thoughts and emotions for a long time, on auto pilot.

"With this in mind, no one can answer your question more truthfully and accurately than you can by using your own criteria. So, I will answer your question with a question. Why would you want to change your life so drastically if you already felt it fulfills you?"

Daisy blushed, "Well, that makes sense again. If a virtuous life leads to fulfillment and I suddenly decided to change my entire life, it would be either because I am not fulfilled with my current lifestyle or because I am about to make a big mistake."

"Exactly. This brings us back to knowing yourself, which becomes much easier to do when you are conscious about what a human life is really about: experiences, thoughts, emotions, decisions, and actions. As Sergio demonstrated with his fruit-and-tree analogy, understanding what being a human really is about can be highly beneficial, regardless of your goals or purpose in life.

"Some people will always try to bully those who are thorough and thoughtful in their decisions and actions. But we should always remember that being over-prepared often leads to success, whereas being under-prepared often leads to failure."

"Yikes! I like that last one," Etienne replied with surprise.

"Let me make sure I understand," I ventured. "We said that each one of these profiles is a collection of behaviors that we often use to describe the people we come to know. Based on what you just said, someone who is self-aware, self-accepting, and thorough in their decision-making, displays a high proficiency in terms of virtuous behaviors. Or, in other words, within their mix of the three behavioral profiles, they are largely virtuous."

"You are close. You cleverly picked up on the three qualities from the examples Daisy and I just went through, but although self-awareness, self-acceptance, and thorough decision-making are qualities that make the virtuous behaviors, they are not the only qualities that fit that profile, and I don't think we can create an exhaustive list of such qualities because they are partially subjective.

"It's better to use this concept of behavioral profiles in a more intuitive way. Think of the people you know—those you would intuitively describe as virtuous, doing the right things, living a fulfilling life, or just being great human beings (not to be confused with naïve human beings). Those are the people you would describe as having a high proficiency in this profile. Then you could think of the qualities they display that lead you to think of them in this way. No one needs to impose their criteria on you; you can derive it by yourself based on the things you appreciate and consider important."

"Makes sense," I replied. "If we both did an analysis of all the people we would describe as highly proficient in virtuous behaviors, we would probably come up with very similar lists of qualities, with a few differences based on our own personal preferences."

"That's right!"

"Great, I think we understand the virtuous behaviors profile. Can we move on to the next one if no one objects?"

"Straight ahead," Tamira confirmed.

> *"Knowing yourself is the beginning of all wisdom." (Aristotle)*

The Ambiguous Behaviors

"Yes, madam! The next set of qualities that often come together are found in the ambiguous behaviors profile. It is very common for people to try to act as if they are on the correct path without really being sure if they are. Some even know that they are not. As humans, we feel bound to give the impression that we know what we are doing."

"That's true!" Etienne jumped in. "I see this everywhere. People who try to show that they don't have any flaws, that they do everything right. As a typical example, you can probably think of a boss, a co-worker, a friend, or a family member who behaves that way. No matter the situation, they have a really hard time admitting their flaws or that they were wrong about something."

Daisy joined in. "That's right. I think that in this same group, we see those who are constantly trying to show how happy they are—the 'look-at-me-I'm-happy!' syndrome. If you observe a little, you can tell that what they show is not what they feel. It can be confusing to distinguish between who is the real deal and who isn't at first. But over time, trying to look perfect raises some pretty big red flags to those who are paying attention."

Andre took the lead back. "You are both right. However, it's important that we don't just look at motive but also at nature. Let me explain… In defense of ambiguousness, we all have strengths and weaknesses, and it is human nature to unwillingly

101

minimize the reality of our weaknesses and sometimes even of our strengths in our own minds. We think, 'I'm special; I'm all strengths; no weaknesses here! Okay, maybe some weaknesses, but so few that I can barely name them.' Sound familiar?"

"That's funny; you bet it sounds familiar! Hardest question to answer in any job interview," Etienne replied, causing some chuckles and comments before Andre continued.

"On the other hand, we also have those who think they have all the weaknesses—the victims of this world, always putting themselves down—or those who always seem to have an excuse for why they let you down instead of owning their failures. I'll say it again, for the most part, we humans have a very difficult time properly identifying our strengths and weaknesses."

"Point made," Daisy said. "By looking at nature as well as motive, you realize that people are not necessarily trying to look one way or another on purpose; it is also in their nature to behave in certain ways, unconsciously."

"Precisely. Human beings can be cunning and deceptive, but we tend to blow these things out of proportion. Most people cannot live a life purely based on calculated deception. Can you imagine living your own life based on deception only? How many calculated lies you would have to make? How many things you would have to constantly account for? You would likely go insane. It would take a psychopath to live such a life, or at least someone deeply entrenched in vicious behaviors.

"Everyone practices deception to different extents, but if you find yourself attributing every event that happens in the world to a deliberate conspiracy or hidden agenda, you are probably giving people more credit than they deserve.

"Most people are genuine most of the time and only practice deception in situations of insecurity, regardless of whether they would accept this publicly or not. Think about yourself, you likely don't practice deception when you are dwelling in an area where you feel confident and have expert authority. There, you usually practice the virtuous behaviors because you want the stuff to be done right! Unless you are a politician or really up to no good and want to take advantage of others, but that's a different story with its own negative effects on yourself."

"So, Andre," I interrupted. "If we compare the ambiguous behaviors to the virtuous behaviors, it feels as if those with a higher proficiency in the virtuous behaviors have a more in-depth understanding of some things about life than those with a higher proficiency in the ambiguous profile."

"That makes sense. The more in-depth your understanding of yourself and your life, or really of anything at all, the less you need to resort to ambiguous tactics to try to wing it or to skim your way through. Think of people you could describe as winging their way through life or some specific stage of it. You will begin to find the qualities that give them a more ambiguous profile and will see the contrast with those who would fall on your virtues bucket."

"I'm liking these behavioral profiles of yours," I said. "I can even see how we could break down the ambiguous profile even further. Some people are genuinely trying to do things the right way but are not sure if they really are. Some people are trying to fake knowing the right things, although they are aware that they are overreaching. They're typically motivated by personal gain, and yes, some people do know what the right and wrong ways are, but still deliberately deceive others to their own advantage. Keep'em coming!"

"That would indeed be a way of diving even deeper. Although, as I process what you just said, I'm not sure I would agree that deliberately deceiving others for our benefit (and at their expense) falls within the ambiguous profile. That one feels more in line with the vicious profile. But I don't think it's worth the fight. The crooked tree could even venture to say that it belongs in the virtuous behaviors, so whatever floats your boat my friend! There is no better judge than the truly conscious self.

"The other two things you mention, however, do definitely fall within ambiguousness. At the core of the ambiguous profile is uncertainty; a higher degree of uncertainty than you are comfortable with. Whether your intentions are to do the right thing or achieve personal gain, a certain degree of uncertainty and overreach is fair game—as long as you are not compromising your integrity.

"We haven't used the ambiguous profile on anyone from our life video library yet, but I think at this point we don't need to—unless anyone wants some more examples."

"I think we are good," Tamira replied. Everyone else nodded.

"If you are out to describe the truth, leave elegance to the tailor."
(Albert Einstein)

104

The Vicious Behaviors

"Alright then. Finally, we have the last, and probably least, of our behavioral profiles, the vicious behaviors. And this time, our unlucky subject is Tom.

"Somehow, Tom has the perfect recipe for disaster, one wrong decision after another; it's like he does it on purpose. He comes out of one hardship or drama only to enter another one, over and over again. Such behavior can be at the root of the same undesirable situations repeating for years, or even for life."

"That sounds quite harsh, but I can relate; I know a few people like that."

Andre smiled. "It's not all fun and games, Tamira. The world has plenty of people who are oblivious to the consequences of their actions, constantly jumping from the current short-term satisfaction to the next one, never bothering to think about even the short-term future or the impact of their actions on those they involve in their blind pursuits."

"But, Andre, although I agree some people are overdramatic or erratic, many people do like to live in the moment or live in the present without worrying too much about the future. Have you ever heard of YOLO, or phrases such as, 'enjoy today because you don't know what tomorrow has in store for you?' Are you saying that if I embraced a philosophy of living in the moment, I would be going in the wrong direction?"

"Great question, Tamira. I wouldn't think so. Based on our definition of a human life, living in the moment would be perfectly aligned with our philosophy here. The understanding that every single day, you will experience events, have thoughts and emotions, make decisions, and take actions would allow you to pause and experience the current moment more profoundly.

"You would feel free from the shackles of overthinking and the pressure of constantly focusing on everything except what is in front of you. You would finally start taking in those experiences and appreciating the thoughts and emotions you get.

"To live in the moment doesn't mean you are on the wrong path. For example, some people link extreme sports to living in the moment. More power to them is my take; they have a higher risk tolerance than I do, that's all.

"Living the moment is about appreciating the present, not about throwing your life away. You can certainly take time to think of what you want your life to be, to know and accept yourself, and then live every moment that comes to you to the fullest while continuing in your chosen direction on your life map. Living in the moment is different from making the same mistakes over and over again."

"Thank you for such a detailed answer. I agree," Tamira replied. So, if we compared the vicious behaviors to the ambiguous behaviors using the same examples from a few minutes ago, could we say that where someone is faking knowledge or purposely misleading others, they are also displaying qualities of the vicious profile?"

106

"That's an interesting observation," Andre conceded. "Yes and no. It would depend on the feelings your decisions and actions create inside of you. Remember, there isn't a manual for any of this. This is all about you living the most fulfilling life you can, which is entirely personal and different for everyone. If you decide to fake that you know something when you don't, you could turn out to be right by chance and end up with a positive result. However, that would have been a gamble and it could have turned out to produce a negative result too.

"The key here is recognizing that you are in a situation whose outcome depends upon whether a gamble that you make pays off. If such a situation rarely occurs, we could probably attribute it to the ambiguous behaviors profile. At the end of the day, no one knows everything about everything, and we are all required to take a gamble or overreach here and there.

"Now, if you constantly find yourself in situations where the outcomes to important developments in your life are based on taking ever-riskier gambles, chances are that something will go terribly wrong at some point and that you are juggling grenades. Such a constant faking of knowledge now makes it a quality of the vicious behaviors profile."

"I see."

"Similarly," he continued. "Purposely misleading others could be a quality found in all three profiles. It all depends on the intention behind it too. In the virtuous profile, it could be because it is necessary for a truly noble purpose that has a very high probability of success and low probability of anything wrong happening—what we might call a white lie, like letting children believe in Santa Claus. In the ambiguous profile, it could be because you are pushing to get somewhere you want to be. Your intentions are still fairly clean, and you still maintain your sense of fulfillment as you engage in your deception—again, a fairly white lie. In the vicious profile, you engage in misleading others for your personal gain, and at their expense, or try to cut corners because you don't want to put in the necessary effort to do things right."

Tamira chimed back in. "It really does feel like the vicious behaviors are the exact opposite of the virtuous ones. If I think of the people I know, who I would describe as mostly displaying vicious behaviors, I can see the gaps in their understanding and acceptance of themselves. I can see the terrible and glaring flaws in some of their decisions and thought processes. It's like they have a blockage that stops them from considering anything other than their biased opinions."

"Enlightening indeed. That's why arguments are usually not productive. The different parties in the argument didn't agree to any rules of engagement, and as a result, both have different criteria regarding what makes a point valid or factual.

"But anyway, we have identified two extremes and a sort of middle point. The extremes are the virtuous and the vicious behaviors. Then, we have the ambiguous middle point, which is a kind of gray area where people try to be on the right track but are not sure if they really are, and if they are, they are not sure how to stay there, so they keep going on and off-track sporadically. This information should be enough for us to understand that there also exists an infinite number of combinations in between those reference points."

I was satisfied with Andre's explanations, as well as a little impatient to be honest, so I blurted, "Brilliant! Can I carry on with your new behavioral profiles concept now?"

"You may proceed," Andre said proudly.

"Dignity does not consist in possessing honors, but in deserving them."
(Aristotle)

The Behaviors in Your Journey

"Now that we have the three behavioral reference points and the objective of keeping people on track, we've enhanced our understanding of how people's journeys develop.

"As life changes continuously and we move from one path to another, some people acquire an edge over the majority by staying longer on the right path and also getting back on track faster. Some give the appearance of having an edge as they figure out their way, and some stay stuck in the wrong paths, repeating the same mistakes.

"We discussed earlier that certain people genuinely live far more satisfying lives than others, regardless of their economic situation. But are they really better off? How can we truly differentiate one from the other? The ambiguous behaviors profile seems to be the most promising for growth in society (as long as you don't overdo it) so is this a fake-it-'til-you-make-it kind of thing, or could there really be ways of living better?"

Etienne attempted an answer, "I wonder if there may be some defining feelings related to being genuinely knowledgeable about the things we talk about, as opposed to giving the appearance that we are, that only each person knows for themselves. If there are, it must be weird to feel like the one faking it, right?

"As I say this, I'm immediately biting my tongue. Yes, the feeling of pretending to know more than we actually do is not better than the feeling of actually knowing without pretension. But at the same time, we have to be realistic. Sometimes it's more about demonstrating confidence than actually knowing stuff. After all, it's only those who think they can do great things that actually do great things. Faking it is just one of the paths that life sometimes requires us to take; it's part of how we learn and become better."

"That's right, Etienne," Andre agreed. "The ambiguous behaviors are not only necessary but also the most appropriate route in some circumstances. It is as much a part of life as the virtuous behaviors. For the most part, life requires us to learn as we go. We don't have time to be fully ready for every situation we encounter or optimally prepared to go in the direction that we want. We just have to deal with life's challenges the best we can as they come. That is why it is impossible for anyone to only exhibit one of the profiles in all areas of their life; we are a mix of all three."

"That's reassuring, to say the least."

Tamira, not yet in full agreement, added her condition, "That all sounds about right. However, we cannot deny that genuine satisfaction is better than apparent satisfaction and also better than no satisfaction. The tricky part is that people often seem to fall into the trap of erroneously convincing themselves that their ambiguousness is actually virtue, and then they get all confused about what is genuine and what is not."

"Also true. Self-awareness is key," Andre considered. "In a similar way, it's one thing to be part of a conversation while you improve your knowledge on a given topic and make connections about it in your own mind—you remain conscious that you don't hold total and complete knowledge about that subject. However, it's quite another thing to convince yourself that you know better about everything than everyone else, and to try to impose your often-incoherent thoughts on others without even trying to understand their perspective or educating yourself.

"All right, I don't know if we will find an answer to this today, but we should start wrapping it up. It's going to be a slow day, but we still have things to do.

"Here is a quick recap,

- We defined life as the experience people go through, which is made of events, thoughts, feelings, decisions, and actions.

- We then said it is important to be aware of this because it allows us to better guide our lives to be more fulfilling.

- We then got into this hypothetical talk about a high-tech library where we can see everything about everyone's lives, which has actually been very helpful in developing our examples.

- The library led to a hypothetical map of life that we can use to see if people are headed in the right direction according to their own thoughts and feelings. This has also lent itself nicely to developing our analogies.

- Next, we discussed the different directions that people take in life.

- These directions led us to realize that some people are headed in the correct direction more often than others

112

and that they also get back on track faster than others when they fall off.

- Talking about those who seemingly do better, led us to discover the concept of behavioral profiles, and we tailored it to our discussion by singling out the virtuous, ambiguous, and vicious behavioral profiles.

- Analyzing the profiles and seeing how they connect with our definition of life and with our life map has helped us uncover some interesting insights into people's behavioral patterns and their reinforcement loops.

"We have made quite some progress today, but I still don't see how hypotheticals will get us the insight we are after. Remember, Sergio? 'The most important factors that lead people to feel fulfilled and live a fulfilling life'…"

"Well, Andre, thank you for the wonderful recap, and I agree we have made a lot of progress. Not only that but I also think we have actually already arrived at our destination. We already have those important factors. You probably didn't realize since you have been focused on defining your behavioral profiles, but we have much more than hypotheticals."

Andre looked puzzled, "How so?"

"You better keep talking!" Daisy threatened.

I smiled. "Unfortunately, we seem to have exhausted our conversation time this morning. It seems we will have to keep the suspense until our next session.

"But you can't tell me this comes as a complete surprise after everything we have discussed! I'm sure you could all smell that we were getting close. Let's use this break to think back through the conversations we've had and search for those important factors. Once we regroup, I believe we will be ready to complete our conversation."

"Fair enough," Andre confirmed. "Let's get to work!"

"When you know a thing, to hold that you know it, and when you do not know a thing, to allow that you do not know it - this is knowledge."
(Confucius)

Application Benefits

Emotional Intelligence

It was a slow day as expected. We found ourselves together again only a few hours later, and we were all eager to continue our talk.

"Alright, Sergio, I think we've waited long enough. It's time you elevate us with your wisdom," Etienne teased.

"Well, it's nothing we don't all know already really, but I think where I can bring value is in helping us all visualize how the knowledge that we've uncovered can be used by others."

"We're listening."

"Let's pick another random person from our life video library. Meet Jason.

"He just turned 20 and is still studying. He wants to become an engineer. Growing up in a middle-class family, not everything has been easy for him. On the bright side, not everything has been hard either. He doesn't consider himself big on reading but enjoys watching series and movies and playing sports and computer games. At the same time as he has been growing and living, Jason has spent 20 years filling up with knowledge to deal with life once it's time for him to become fully independent.

"Given the opportunity of mentoring Jason, we would be able to share the insights we have gained with him. Obviously, the longer our mentoring relationship, the more we would be able to connect with him and guide him to understand a collection of important things.

"We would start by letting Jason in on a secret: We would tell him that we know what his life has been about, is about, and always will be about; that actually, we know this for every single person on Earth. His obvious reaction will be skepticism.

"We will then challenge him to define a human life, just like we challenged ourselves. It's not important that he succeeds in putting together a complete answer in a short amount of time; what matters is that he tries. Since we know what a human life is about, it will be very easy for us to see the gaps in his definition and ask him about those without just giving him the answer.

"As tempting as it may be, it is of the utmost importance that we don't reveal our secret too quickly—i.e. before Jason can appreciate the effort that went into putting it together. Giving the answer too quickly may trigger him into thinking that there was nothing to it and that it's not important. Jason needs to struggle at least a little so that he can formulate proof in his own mind that what he is about to learn doesn't come easy and that he doesn't just have to take our word for it. We want Jason to seek the knowledge as opposed to us just blurting it out. Remember, Jason just turned 20. He has no idea that many people who are 30, 40, even 60 are still not aware of this stuff.

"Through questions and examples, we would guide Jason to reach our definition of a human life, which is that he will keep living different experiences and events; he will have thoughts and emotions about everything he comes into contact with; he will make thousands, millions of decisions, and take unquantifiable actions every day until he dies, regardless of where he's at in life.

"Once he accepts our definition or tweaks it to make his own definition while maintaining our basic meaning, we will have created a basis of understanding life that we will be able to build upon. We can now provide Jason with the tools that he will be able to use to live a more fulfilling life."

Etienne, consciously simulating the behavior of a good and attentive student, lifted his hand.

"Yes, Etienne?"

"What if Jason comes up with a totally different definition of what a human life is and doesn't accept ours?"

"Very simple. If his definition defeats ours through logic, practicality, and realism, then we should either adopt his definition or update ours to incorporate or remove ideas as necessary. On the other hand, if it is clear to us that Jason's definition doesn't measure up to ours, it is our duty as mentors to guide Jason to the correct one through probing questions and empathy. All this with the understanding that some people cannot be saved, no matter how many life floats you throw at them. A mentorship relationship is a two-way street. If both parties are not engaged, it dies."

"Fair enough," Etienne agreed.

"Perfect, so now that our philosophy of what a human life is about, is aligned with Jason's, we can share with him examples like that of Jane losing her job. It's important that we guide him to understand that even though negative events will happen in his life, his feelings about himself should be tied to how he handles the situation and not to the negative situation itself. We want to show him that if he can remain conscious about this inescapable process during important events in his life, his journey will become far less complex, and he will be able to make better decisions because he won't let his emotions take over the reins.

"By being conscious about this process, he won't live on autopilot, letting his unconscious alone define his path. His decision-making strength will benefit from both his unconscious intuition and his conscious thought. Not only will he be open to accepting both insights, but he will also eventually expect to clearly understand both and reconcile them—or at least make sure they don't contradict each other when an important decision needs making."

"Can you give an example of these two insights contradicting each other?" Tamira asked.

"Sure can. A typical example of a contradiction between your unconscious intuition and your conscious thought could be when your internet or cable provider calls you near the end of your yearly contract to tell you that they have 'great offers.'

"Your intuition immediately kicks in to tell you that they are probably just trying to raise your monthly cost. For some reason, these great offers never have a lower price tag than what you are currently paying; it's a great mystery. But at the same time as you are expecting this yearly game they play, your conscious thought tells you, 'Well, if there is a better offer than what I have right now, maybe I should listen.'

"You may then decide to listen to them rather than flushing them off, in order to formulate your conscious thought. If they do indeed have a deal that you consider good for you and you go for it, which does happen on occasion, then you reconciled your thoughts toward your conscious decision making. If it's the typical sales pitch with no real added benefit to you and you decide to tell them you are not interested, then you reconciled your thoughts toward your intuition."

"That makes sense. Thank you," Tamira replied. "I'm thinking that being aware of this process would also help Jason balance his emotions and rational thoughts better during rough times. By understanding that events trigger thoughts and emotions, Jason would be more aware that important events can trigger strong emotions, temporarily clouding his judgment. If he made it a personal rule to wait and reconcile his thoughts and emotions in a similar way to the one you've just described, he would also make better decisions."

"It could also help him avoid some of the ugly mistakes that a lack of emotional intelligence causes people to make so often," Etienne replied thoughtfully. "I would've probably avoided a few bad ones myself if someone had managed to help me understand this better when I was younger."

"Indeed my friend," I replied. "Which brings all the more value to these things we know and can share with those willing to listen and think about them."

He nodded.

"So, moving on, Jason would likely ask clarifying questions, like Tamira just did. This is where we could tailor our insights to fit within his life experiences and understanding of life.

"We have to remember that no matter what we say and how we say it, it is impossible that our message will reach everyone the same way. We have to be familiar enough with our knowledge to include it in examples that our mentee can relate to. If we guide Jason correctly, he will come to understand that this process is critical in both positive and negative experiences because they can kick him off track and play with his mental health.

"By the same token, if Jason does accept our definition and internalizes it, which I am confident he will—I mean if Andre fell for the fruit and the tree analogy..."

"Yeah, yeah, yeah!" Andre shouted.

I laughed. "...Once he accepts our definition, he will realize that life is no longer a race against everyone. Any comparative thoughts of whether he is good enough versus anyone else will become less important, because his fulfillment is based on internal factors he can control, rather than external ones. He will also make fewer rushed decisions which should translate into less chaos in his life.

"He will see life as a series of events that happen, where he feels certain things, has thoughts, makes decisions, and takes actions. He will learn to base his self-worth, his confidence, and his feelings of fulfillment on the parts of the process that he can control. This will bring him peace because his feelings about himself will be disconnected from outside influence."

As usual, Andre brought a touch of realism. "I like how perfect that sounds, but let's be honest here, there aren't enough words that we could say to Jason for his self-confidence not to take the occasional hit, or for him to not make the odd rash decision here and there."

"I completely agree. Our conversation didn't just turn us into super-humans. Just like Jason, none of us will be perfect by being aware of all this. We will make mistakes too; we will find ourselves focusing on the wrong things sometimes, and sadly, we will realize that some vicious behaviors we have gotten accustomed to are hard to let go of.

"In those cases however, we will have cultivated the mental ability to understand that those things will continue to happen. By expecting them, we will be faster at identifying situations that send us off track and to course-correct when we are drifting off. Internalizing the knowledge we have built through our conversations keeps us aware that if we want to stay on track—if we truly want to feel the fulfillment that can be felt in life—we have to regularly monitor ourselves.

"We won't be perfect at it, but the more we do it, the quicker we will get at correcting our route and at staying on the right track, and so will Jason.

"The beauty of understanding this process is that you don't need anyone to tell you what is right or wrong. This knowledge allows you to simply pull it from within you through sheer self-awareness and by constantly going after fulfillment. As you said, it is easier said than done and we *will* make mistakes. This is fine and to be expected. What matters is that we immediately correct ourselves and try to do better next time.

"Sounds fair; I can get behind that," Andre replied.

"It is very important to understand that emotional intelligence is not the opposite of intelligence; it is not the triumph of heart over head; it is the unique intersection of both."
(David Caruso)

You Can Change the Past

"Glad we agree, Andre," I said. "Remember I mentioned how we may not actually need the high-tech video library to exist when we started our deep dive into this?"

"I do."

"Well, it turns out it was a good risk to take. Jason already has the life video of himself in his own mind, so we are just making him aware that it's there and that he can use it. He can look at anything that has happened during his life to identify where he may have been right or wrong.

"He will know that as time goes on, he will gain a better understanding of himself as a human being, of those around him, and of the world in general. Armed with this new understanding, he will be able to go back to these memories as many times as he needs. These explorations can bring him new insights, and even closure to unfortunate events so that he can liberate his mind to focus on more prosperous thoughts."

Daisy didn't sound convinced. "That wouldn't be as precise as the high-tech video library where we have all the information though. If we reach into our minds for our own life video, we won't remember what our exact thoughts were every second of our lives."

"That's a fair point," I answered. "However, I am not sure it makes much of a difference once we add some perspective."

"What do you mean?"

"Well, imagine for yourself. You are Daisy, and I just pulled your life video from our high-tech library—"

"Oh no! Should I be worried?" Daisy said half-jokingly, half shocked.

"No need to worry," I smiled. "Can you imagine the effort it would require for me to analyze one important event in your life using the life video library? I would have to reach into your thoughts, consider everything happening in your life at that time, understand your values, the things you like and don't like, and so much more. I would need a high-tech video library to investigate you and a *lot* of time.

"On the other hand, if you were to look into yourself for that same event, the speed at which your mind works to recall your own experience and mix it with your knowledge of yourself and your understanding of life would be unmatchable. You wouldn't want to dwell in all the detail of your life video library even if you had this technology, because you really wouldn't need to; you lived through your own experience."

"That makes sense, but what if I can't remember the events clearly, like if my memory is foggy or I just remember flashes of the event?"

"That's just a human limitation. I think we need to be a little practical here. If all you remember are flashbacks, then that's just how it is for that specific memory; that's all you get. Imagine remembering everything that ever happened in your life perfectly? How tragic would it be to have a perfect recollection of all negative events? No thanks!

"What's more, you won't have the same amount of detail for all your memories: some will be blurry, others crystal clear. You would have to take it up with the manager to change that," I joked, pointing up.

"But on the bright side, every time you gain new insights into yourself, of human beings in general, or of the world you live in, you can always go back, take another look at some of those memories that just won't leave you alone, and apply your new understanding."

"And why would I be interested to keep going back into my memories?" Daisy asked.

"Because that's just what we humans do! You're going to tell me that you don't find yourself revisiting old memories in your mind: some good, some bad, and some that you haven't come to terms with? We all do. I think I even recall you mentioning a few days ago that you came to terms with some old memories or something like that. Are you pulling my leg?"

"Fine, fine, I'll cut you some slack," Daisy replied in a playful voice. "I was just pressure-testing your logic; I am in full agreement. Actually, more than in agreement, I think we can add one more insight to Jason's toolbox that stems from the life video library."

"You had me there for a second, but don't make us anxious; let's hear that insight!" I said.

"The thought actually occurred to me back to when I mentioned that I came to terms with some memories. I realized that I was actually able to change the past."

Andre sounded discouraged as he lifted his gaze. "Please tell me you're not about to come up with an imaginary time machine now."

"Oh no, leave those to Sergio! Imagine this scenario: Something happened in your past and you understood that event in a certain way that made you upset. Say, a friend let you down in a way that you didn't expect. Several years pass, and your thoughts about that event keep bothering you.

"But, as we discussed earlier, people grow and reach stages where they understand things that they didn't understand before. So, at some point, you gain some new insight or understanding of life that allows you to look back at that event from a different, improved perspective based on your newfound knowledge.

"Once you take a look at the same event from this new perspective, you come to realize things that you were not aware of before due to your lack of understanding at the time. With this newfound clarity, you come to realize that although it seemed like your friend let you down, in reality, they let themselves down even more; they tried to not let you down at their own expense but still failed and ended up hurting you."

"This new perspective could have been gained by learning new information about that event—information you were unaware of before—or thanks to an improved understanding of human behavior and of people's emotions. The new perspective makes it so that while still negative, the event is not as dramatic anymore and bothers you less because you now understand it and accept it better.

"I'm aware that the past cannot be changed in the literal sense, but what really matters to us is our perspective of the past.

"When you think of an event in your past, you are not viewing it from the same detached perspective you would be if you were watching a history documentary, where some random person let another random person down. You are thinking about that event from your perspective. You have emotions and thoughts attached to it that affect you to this day; your friend let you down. If that perspective changed, wouldn't it have the effect of changing the past for you? If the emotions and thoughts that get triggered by that memory changed and you had to tell the story of that event, wouldn't that story change too?"

"Wow, I think you are right; it would!" I replied. When someone hurts us, we tend to get on fighting mode. We see them as this evil being who consciously and with the worst intentions did us harm, but even though wicked people who do bad things do exist, they are hardly the norm. More often than not, people hurt you out of ignorance and not out of evil intent. I can see how understanding that someone's ignorance and not wickedness was at the root of the issue would impact my emotions related to that event. I agree that we can change the past in our minds by improving our understanding of it!"

"Reality is created by the mind; we can change our reality by changing our mind." (Plato)

127

Your Journey

"Alright. Now that we've introduced Jason to the life video library and showed him how he can make use of his continuous intellectual growth to better understand the past, then if we pursue our original thought process, it naturally follows that we tell him about the Life Map.

"We would tell him that he can create a map of his life in his own mind. He can look at it at any time to see if he is moving in the correct direction according to his own thoughts.

"Remember, after understanding what the life of every person is really about, our goal has been to use this information to identify the most important factors that lead people to feel fulfilled and live a fulfilling life. During our exploration, we dismissed the idea of a master formula because everyone's life is different, and we are not trying to create a dogma or judge what is good versus evil. We want to give everyone tools to decide their own path, beliefs, and values, regardless of what they are.

"Although the life video library and the life map sound like impossible technologies, do not actually exist, and are not likely to ever exist as material things, they do already exist inside the mind of every one of us. If they didn't until today, it is fairly easy for us to create them right now, on the spot, just by becoming aware of them. There lies one of the incredible abilities of the human mind."

"You are cunning indeed," Andre replied. "We didn't need the science fiction stuff after all. You were just using it to pass on the concept. I must say I'm impressed with the depth of your vision."

"I apologize if you feel a little misled. Sometimes, we need to remove the barriers of what we consider possible by using a little 'savoir-faire' to find answers to questions that are elusive, such as the one we have been discussing.

"But I'm not finished yet, because we have more information for Jason! If there is one key factor to living a more fulfilling life, it is to stay tuned to the destinations he picks in his map of life—his calling, his objectives, his values, whatever Jason wants to call them. In other words, to stay on the correct path and get back on track as fast as possible anytime he falls off track.

"We are letting Jason know that it's okay to change his direction towards a new destination at any time, as long as he gets on track toward whichever destination he wants to go."

"Question here," Tamira intervened. "How is it okay to change paths? This whole time I have been thinking that changing paths is wrong; it means you've wasted time on the old path and didn't know what you were doing in the first place."

"Fair point again. Let's remind ourselves of what the direction of the correct path is. Do you remember?"

"The correct path is what makes Jason feel fulfilled as he goes along it," she said. "As I answer your question, it suddenly makes sense. It's okay to change direction because there is no point in following a direction that is no longer fulfilling."

"There you have it," I replied. "Not only that, but a concept that keeps coming up is that as time passes, we grow and gain a new understanding of ourselves. As we attain new knowledge, we are destined and should expect to change directions several times during our lives in different areas and we have talked about how we can measure the impact of these changes."

"Ah, you are right; I remember. The better you know and accept yourself, the less knee-jerk adjustments you will need to make, and the further the new direction from the current one, the bigger the change," Tamira quoted.

"You got it," I concluded. "We also talked about how everyone's correct path is different and unique, regardless of their upbringing, like for the twin sisters I mentioned before.

"The correct path for Jason could actually be to go in one direction—to become a lawyer, for example. Then, as he gains new insights about himself and about life, his correct path could be to decide that what he really wants to do for a living is to own a farm and grow fruits and vegetables."

"That's a pretty drastic change when it comes to careers," Etienne commented.

"You bet it is. But the only thing that matters is that Jason goes where he feels fulfilled. What he probably wouldn't know yet, as he is making the decision to become a farmer, is that in the future, he will likely be able to combine the two fields he knows well, law and agriculture, to make a positive change in the world that few people would be able to make, due to the unique combination of his specialties.

"This is where it's important that Jason knows himself the best he can, and this includes knowing what a human life is about. That way, no external opinion can have more weight than his call to fulfillment. No one on our planet has a manual that says that if you do one thing, you cannot do another. No one has a universal manual for success or fulfillment. Jason holds everything he needs within himself. All he needs to do is to dedicate the time to listen to his best self and to stay true to himself.

"Even more, by using examples like that of Jane's being directionally correct during the hardship of losing her job, we will reassure him that staying on track doesn't need to entail living a stressful life, always taking the highway toward his objectives. Today, he can pick the route he likes, even if it's a little slower. Tomorrow, he can pick the route with the scenery, which is also slower but beautiful, because he is sharing it with a loved one. The day after, he can take the highway because he feels energized. Going in the right direction doesn't mean becoming a slave to his objectives; it means cherishing his way there and to keep moving forward."

"Wow," Daisy said. "We really did talk about all these things. It makes me feel as though life should be looked at as a journey where we should expect both good and challenging times from the get-go; where we don't only have to savor our moments of delight but also many of the difficult moments. We just need to look at them with curiosity and resolve rather than anger or apprehension.

"It's a journey where anything can happen, and we get to pick our direction as we face the many trials we find in our way; a journey where things often have a way of working out in ways we least expect if we have a little faith in ourselves."

"Beautifully put, Daisy. Life is a journey indeed. If we are always on our way to certain destinations, let those be destinations that we consciously chose and not ones that indifference chose for us."

"Another good one there, Sergiocrates," Etienne joked, and everyone laughed.

"Your direction is more important than your speed."
(Richard L. Evans)

Self-Awareness

"Thanks, Etienne, I'll take that one as a compliment. But let's continue, because there's one more thing for us to tell Jason about, that there is a vast spectrum of traits and behaviors he can embrace or internalize along the way—the vicious, ambiguous, and virtuous behaviors. We would tell him that these sets of behavior tend to come bundled together. That even if it's not easy to explain, or if it sounds judgmental, that others can identify the dominant behavioral patterns in him as much as he can identify them in others.

"Some common examples that we can probably all relate to are:

- The friend who is fun to have around but is unreliable.

- The friend who is a really good listener.

- The friend who is polarizing.

- The friend who is genuinely always trying to help.

- The friend who doesn't let anyone else talk.

- The friend who thinks they know everything but can never back it up.

- The friend who will never concede they are wrong or that your idea is better.

- The friend who is always positive.

- The friend who is always negative.

- The friend who is always trying to have the situation lean their way.

- The friend who doesn't have a hidden agenda.

- The friend who always seems to understand what is going on.

"Etcetera, you get the point. Is it judgmental? Probably. But it doesn't make it any less true that we all have these thoughts. Even though we may give people the benefit of the doubt more often than they deserve, we see these patterns in others, and notice the behaviors that those close to us have chosen to adopt."

"It's funny you mention those examples," Etienne commented. "As you were going through them, you were triggering pictures in my mind of people I know. I actually have a friend who is super negative but thinks he is positive just because he is enthusiastic."

"That's a good observation too. People can be confused about the behaviors they display because they lack understanding of themselves and others—a gap in self-awareness and emotional intelligence. It's important that we guide Jason to understand that there can be a difference between the image he thinks he is projecting, and the image others are perceiving.

"If he is able to take a good cold look at himself from an outsider's perspective, he will be able to see the gaps between the two perspectives and adjust his behavior as he considers it necessary. If he rejects this proposition, he is destined to not understand why people see him a certain way, or to not even be aware that people see him a certain way."

Tamira wasn't convinced. "This is interesting, but can you help me connect it to how it allows Jason to live a more fulfilled life?" she asked. "This seems a little superficial; like it's more about appearances than fulfillment. Some people don't care about what others think of them and it doesn't make them any less fulfilled. How does this apply to them too?"

"Great point indeed," I replied. "That's an observation with multiple facets worth examining. Are you calling into question the link between self-awareness and fulfillment, or how we're defining self-awareness?"

She responded, "I think the link between self-awareness and fulfillment became very clear when Andre described the virtuous behavioral profile and used Silvia as the virtuous example. What I find a little off here, is the assumption that Jason cares about what others think of him and that this impacts his sense of fulfillment."

"Thank you for that," I said. "This helps me channel the answer to your question, though it may not be easy, I think we can get to an agreement."

"It's worth the try," she accepted.

"Great. So, I think we should breakout self-awareness into two pieces to isolate the one we are challenging. In this case the first piece is at the personal level, your awareness of yourself in relationship to yourself, and second piece is at the social level, your awareness of yourself in relationship to other people.

"At the personal level, as you mentioned, we are all on the same page. The behaviors Jason chooses to adopt impact his sense of fulfillment. If he behaves in ways that are inconsistent with what he considers to be right or what he considers to be important, he won't feel as fulfilled. This happens to all of us in one way or another.

"As an example, think of all the times you've had that extra cookie, extra drink, or that especially unhealthy meal you were craving. Remember the feeling of satisfaction as you were having it and the immediate guilt right after? That is a feeling of unfulfillment—if that's even a word. A feeling that you went against yourself."

"Story of my life," Daisy commented.

I continued with a smile, "In contrast, think of that time when you didn't feel like working out, but you still did it. Remember how satisfying it was after, and how you felt good about yourself? It wasn't because you became fit in a single workout session; it was because you worked out. You did the right thing, and it felt good.

"Just like in those two examples, your behavioral profiles impact every area of your life. We've all treated someone in a way we have later felt ashamed of and someone else in a way we feel proud of. We've all found ourselves in a sticky situation where we behaved in ways inconsistent with our ideals, causing us unwanted emotions. By consciously choosing the behavioral ideals we want to live by and respecting them, we align with our correct path and live more fulfilling lives."

"So far so good," Tamira approved.

"Your quarrel is with the social level of self-awareness," I ventured. "This piece is more complex because the behaviors you want to adopt may be in opposition to what is considered socially acceptable, and because there will always be social pressure to repeat and accept a series of ideas and 'mainstream mottos' that are often unrealistic. You propose that whether Jason cares or not about what others think of him doesn't make him more or less fulfilled."

She agreed, "That's right, I'm seeing fulfillment as a personal and internal thing. If he doesn't care, he doesn't care... As we've said before, Jason is the best judge of himself."

"I see... I'm aware people often say they don't care of what others think about them; this is indeed one of those mainstream mottos I just referred to. But in reality, that statement cannot simultaneously be true and a source of fulfillment. That type of statement is typically rooted in buried negative feelings from events a person experienced, it's a way to divert from painful emotions that are not fulfilling. People can lie to themselves all they want by repeating that they don't care about things they obviously should, it doesn't make it any more real or less immature. Carelessness does not lead to fulfillment. It's an oxymoron to say I am fulfilled because I don't care."

Tamira signaled to keep going.

"Humans are social beings. We all care to some extent about how others perceive us. That's why we dress a certain way or adopt certain behaviors. Even if Jason said he doesn't care about how others see him, by those same words, he would also be silently saying that he doesn't want to be perceived as someone who cares about how others see him. That rabbit hole can run deep, but simply asking a few deeper questions to those 'careless' people will uncover the truth. Just identify things they actually do care about, and then tell them you perceive them as the opposite of that, it probably won't sit well, even if they do a great job at attempting to hide it."

"Wow, that's pretty strong there," Tamira replied. "Although I don't disagree with you, I can still see how Jason can still just answer your probes with, 'I told you I don't care what you think about me.' How would you handle that?"

"Well, I would first consider whether it's worth my time to handle that," I laughed. "I'm equally aware that many people don't really mean they don't care about how others see them when they say exactly that. It's one of those things where the popular phrase doesn't exactly mean what the words say. Their meaning is often more in terms of not caring that some, or that even most people see them in a negative way because of certain behaviors they have chosen to adopt.

"For example, the good person cares about being perceived as good by those close to them but doesn't make a fuss if strangers don't see them in the same light. They understand that someone who is not close to them is not likely to have an accurate perception of who they are. In this case, even though someone would typically say, I don't care of what others think about me, the real meaning is somewhere along the lines of, I don't care of what strangers think about me."

"That's a slight difference, but is it that important?" She asked.

"To be sure, I'm not trying to nitpick on unnecessary details," I said. "The issue lies in the continuous repeating of incorrect, 'I don't care' ideas. It has many people confused about what they are really trying to say and of what the extent of their 'I don't careism' is. People have gotten into the habit of just constantly blurting out 'I don't care' to hide from reality without paying attention to what they are saying."

Andre chuckled, "Add to this that people also find it difficult to go back on their word after they've voiced something, and you have a beautiful recipe for incoherent and illogical discussion."

"Exactly!" I replied. "People repeat absurd popular mottos, they then feel the need to defend their irrational position because confidence good, going back on your word, bad. Then, they end up digging a deeper hole into their own self-made deception, rather than admitting they spoke without base. Many people carry an internal conflict that lasts for years and sometimes for life, of unconsciously trying to adhere to flimsy, contradicting philosophies they defended more than they should have…"

"That's close to how I see it too," Daisy added. "In the context of someone saying they don't care about what others think of them, I think that if they can really mean it and find that it brings them fulfillment, then as Andre would say, all power to them. It's just hard to buy the dismissive, 'I don't care' excuse most people use out of habit.

"From personal experience, I can think back to a couple of times I've used it myself. It's typically in a situation where I don't want to go into the details and don't want to call attention to what my emotions are on the subject. But I have to agree that even though I may have said I don't care what they think about me, it wasn't really true. I guess as long as we stay conscious that our I don't cares are just a temporary screen, we would avoid that self-deception Sergio mentioned."

"That makes sense," I said, as I looked towards Tamira. "We've beaten around the bush a little bit, but I think I may just have found the silver bullet while Daisy was talking!"

"Give it your best shot!" Tamira mused.

"When someone says they don't care about how others see them, are they also implying they don't care about the impact they have on others, even a little?"

"It seems they would imply that, yes..." she replied.

"In that case, intuitively, would you expect to hear those words from someone who feels fulfilled or someone who feels defeated?"

"Ouch! I have to say, defeated. When I think of fulfillment, it's a good feeling which includes wanting others to also feel it. It doesn't make sense to me that someone who feels that good would not care even a little about spreading the love."

"So, it seems as if at the social level, claiming to not care in any way of how others perceive us, is more of a symptom that something is not right in the person's fulfillment wheelhouse," I concluded.

"I think we are in agreement after all," she accepted. "Self-awareness at both the personal and social levels, lead to a higher sense of fulfillment."

"Perfect, I'm glad we got through that!" I added with relief. "Then, for the sake of self-awareness, Jason will be looking out for his patterns of behaviors when he looks at his own life video. Once he finds them, he will decide which ones he wants to move forward with and which ones to leave behind. He will then fit the good ones into his life map with the understanding that these behaviors impact him personally and socially.

"All right ladies and gents, this is it. As much as I've enjoyed our conversation and could keep on adding benefits Jason would acquire from our mentorship, I think anything more would just be overshadowed by what we've already discussed.

"To conclude, we've provided Jason with the answer to what life is about without imposing any ideology of what is right, wrong, good, and evil.

"We've given him a solid platform to build on. One based on reality and on the undeniable characteristics that make him human. A platform that is moldable to his current understanding of himself, and which he can improve and update as he grows as a person.

"And finally, we've revealed the existence of his internal compass and showed him how to always set it towards fulfillment.

"Jason has all he needs to discover himself, find his purpose, and consistently move in the right direction.

"What is necessary to change a person is to change his awareness of himself." (Abraham Maslow)

Ж

Part Two: Introspection

The Journey

Welcome to the second part of the book! The space dialogue in which you just took part has now ended. After Sergio's conclusion, everyone voiced their agreement and felt satisfied with the outcome of the conversation. In this second part, we will go over some reflective questions and practical guidance that can help you internalize the book's insights in your life.

If you are reading this, you are the beneficiary of a life, of being alive. What this means is that:

- You have the opportunity of living through all kinds of experiences, both good and bad.

- You have the ability to feel emotions and have thoughts about all your experiences and everything that you become aware of.

- You have the power of making decisions and taking actions based on those thoughts and emotions.

You will do these things your entire life. You cannot fight it; you cannot stop it; these things will happen whether you want them to or not.

As you can see in Image 3, emotions and thoughts are on the same step. This is because you may feel like some situations will trigger your emotions first, while other situations may trigger your thoughts first. It doesn't matter which comes first; they both just happen, and none of us have any say in it.

Image 3

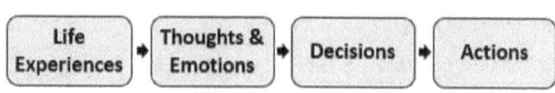

Seeing life as a journey is the ability to understand and appreciate our human life for what it is at its core, not just the things we acquire, accumulate, or become accustomed to while alive.

Notice that I said, "Not only the things we acquire." Our possessions and customs can make us appreciate life too, but they can only get us so far. They are not enough to make us feel fulfilled. Truly feeling fulfilled requires understanding and acceptance of the things that go on inside us, the things that no one else can see.

The examples of people who are considered rich, religious, prodigious, or successful but unhappy and unfulfilled are abundant enough to make the point that no accomplishment by itself brings you fulfillment without your own internal "approval stamp."

Many of the wrong turns people take in life are due to being unaware of this process. In Image 4, you will see an area labeled as your area of control. This does not mean that you have zero control over your life experiences; you do have some control since your actions will lead to experiences. What is most

146

important is how you deal with any of your life experiences, how you handle your area of control.

Image 4

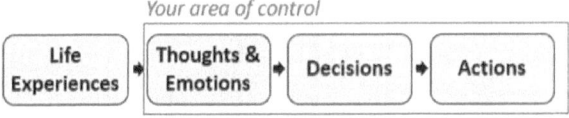

A very common mistake people make is that they leave one of the areas on autopilot. Imagine the impact that neglecting any of these steps can have on your life. Imagine jumping straight from life experience to action, without paying attention to your thoughts, emotions, or decisions. I'm sure you can picture instances where you've done just that, and you can also picture people close to you who have done the same.

You may feel like this definition of life is in competition with whatever you may consider important in life—like you have to choose between this definition and the things you feel are important in your life. You do not. Whatever your goals are, whatever you consider important, consciously understanding this process will make you better at it. You can re-read The Fruit and The Tree chapter if you want to revisit an example of this.

Also, when thinking about life, avoid falling into the trap of unnecessary nitpicking. We don't need a perfectly exact definition of a human life to understand it, just one that is accurate and practical.

For example, it would be easy to argue that emotions and thoughts are not part of your area of control, and in some

147

ways, you would be correct. However, right after you get those thoughts and emotions that fall out of your control, you come to face the thoughts and emotions within your control. If you prefer to look at it that way, feel free to do so.

No one has a monopoly over how much detail is good enough. You can even expand this process further, make it shorter, or add things that you consider should be part of it—as long as you truly believe they should and are not lying to yourself. The images that follow are examples of how our definition can easily be expanded or contracted.

Image 5: Expanded

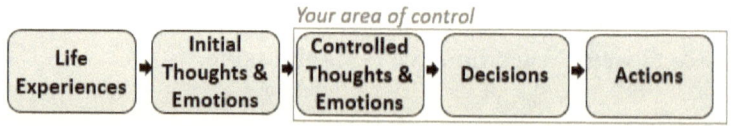

Image 6: Contracted

"*Life is really simple, but we insist on making it complicated.*"
(*Confucius*)

Your Life Video

Take a moment to get ready to look at your life in the comfort and privacy of your mind, to access the areas that no one else can see and that you don't want anyone to see. The areas where only you know the truth, even though you are used to playing the ambiguous tactics for others because they would never understand, or because it would just be too much to explain.

Before you start, you must know that even though you cannot physically change the past, your knowledge and understanding of the world grows every single day, and therefore, you can understand the past differently today from how you did at the time. This means that even though you cannot change the past physically, you can change your understanding of it, which may improve how you feel about it.

The questions that follow are not meant to be a complete guide to creating your life video—and no complete guide exists. They are just the spark to get you thinking about it, just enough to get you started. The idea here is to help you realize that you can look at your life video with any question, at any time, and to get a true answer from yourself to yourself.

Experiences

I know something about you. You've had positive and negative experiences that you think about quite often—unless you live an extremely busy life with no time to sit down and think for a few minutes, that is.

If you're going to delve into negative past experiences, you might as well do it with the purpose of understanding them, rather than simply re-running an endless loop of the same stuff that bothers you. Dramatic emotions can be addictive and are not good for you in high doses.

Thinking back to positive experiences on the other hand is a good source of uplift, but you must be careful not to live in the comfort of some good old memories, while neglecting your present and future.

Here are some questions to try to recall some of these memories:

- Can you think of some experiences you are proud of?

- Can you think of some experiences you are not proud of and that you caused?

- Can you think of some experiences you had no control over that brought you sorrow?

- Can you think of some positive and negative experiences that happened by sheer luck?

- Can you think of your life experiences in general—where you grew up, traveled to, people you grew up with, etc.?

Remember, this life video is yours and yours alone. All of your actions are tied to decisions that are tied to emotions and thoughts.

The better you can reconstruct them by accepting the comfortable and uncomfortable realities that come with them, the more you can learn from them. Don't simply force your experiences through some cookie-cutter 'feel-good' mold, that protects you from the reality that you do wrong things and that you fall off track too.

Simultaneously, don't overly blame yourself for every bad thing that has happened. The whole point of this is to look at yourself and to accept yourself with your qualities and flaws. You are not the only one who has lived through problems and unfortunate events; everyone has. By simply being able to read these words, you can rest assured that there are millions of people who are going through harder times than you are at this exact moment.

Emotions

Sometimes, as we go through life and time passes, we realize that a few years have passed since we were our 'old self', and we see how we have changed, or how we have not changed.

- Can you think of some emotions you felt in the past but have rejected for long periods of time?

  - For example, some people reject the emotion of envy. The moment they feel it, they close themselves to it because they know it is a harmful emotion. Other people reject the emotion of love after going through a traumatic event.

- Can you think of some emotions that keep hurting you over the long term and you may have been accepting for too long?

  - Envy is a good example here as well. Have you been accepting it for too long? How about indecisiveness? Have you been neglecting important decisions in your life that keep causing you negative feelings? The only way to permanently change these emotions is to deal with them.

- Can you think of some negative emotions that you may have experienced regularly, which you know are not good and disapprove of, but that since no one can see them, no one can know and so you haven't felt the need to block them?

- For example, deeply rooted and almost unconscious superiority complex, inferiority complex, or silent racism are prevalent in today's society.

- Can you think of some emotions that you make an effort to bring into your life because you know they are good for you?

  - For example, you can try to conjure calm emotions by breathing deeply and slowly, or happy emotions by not just looking at the negative aspects of bad situations but also at the hidden positive side of things.

- Can you think of a time when you did something so well, where you put in a lot of effort, and it made you feel like you completely 'nailed it?'

  - Can you recall the emotions that led you to it? You may want to replicate those as often as you can.

One thing about destructive emotions such as anger or rage is that when we are feeling them, we feel righteous—like we are right to feel that way because an incredible wrong has been done to us. We go on to break things or say hurtful things. But then, when the heat passes, we feel kind of dumb. When we look in retrospect, we often feel ashamed of our behavior, even though most would never admit it.

As you can probably imagine, if you can relate to this, you will feel destructive emotions again at some point. You can't stop it; your life will not be perfect. Think of what you can do when you feel the emotions to allow them to cool down without taking those rushed actions.

Another thing about strong emotions, such as the euphoria of falling in love, or the seductive nature of someone we admire, is that they can blind us.

How many times have you heard the story of the person who seemed good but ended up being bad? If someone deceives you, it may not be entirely their fault. As harsh as it sounds, you likely played a role in your own deception throughout most of these situations by having unrealistic expectations. Be good, not naïve...

A simple way to know if you are being blinded by positive emotions is to try to find the negative qualities in the person you like or admire. Not the negative qualities that are really positive qualities in disguise, like the ones you give at your job interviews; I'm talking about the real negative qualities that you see and say, "Hmmm, this person is nice and all, but they do this thing which I don't like," without trying to excuse their behavior.

Of course, this emotional blindness not only applies to positive emotions; it also applies to negative ones. Nobody is purely evil or purely good. Even that person you don't like is loved by someone else for one reason or another. If all you can see is only the good or only the bad, you can bet your money that you are being blinded by your emotions and your decision-making potential is being hindered by them.

Emotionally intelligent people make the effort to take a step back and look at things from a different perspective.

Thoughts

- Can you think of instances where overthinking made things worse?

- Can you think of instances where the lack of interest, attention, or thinking about it made things worse?

- Can you recall instances where you took the time to think about a challenging situation a little more and you found a better answer or better ways of dealing with the situation?

- If you were being 100% honest with yourself, would you consider your thoughts until today to be mostly positive, negative, defensive, aggressive, victimizing (with you as the victim), virtuous, or non-virtuous?

  - Are you happy with your result? If not, what do you think you need to do to change it? Remember, this is all in your mind. No point in lying to yourself. Should you try the question again?

- Can you think of instances where you knew the right thing to do, but still did the wrong thing? How did you feel after? How do you feel about it now?

- Vice-versa, can you think of instances where you thought of the right thing to do and did it, despite pressure to do the wrong thing? How did you feel after? How do you feel now?

- Based on the last two questions, can you feel the long-lasting effect your actions have on you?

Something I have realized is that most people stop thinking too quickly. I'm not advocating for overthinking here but against not thinking enough. I see this situation all the time when an issue arises, or when someone is trying to make an important, but difficult decision.

People think a little bit; they ask a few questions, and *bam*! They make the decisions with whatever they could muster in those two minutes. They then go on to call themselves decisive, efficient, or whatever rocks their world. Then, more often than not, they hit a brick wall because they didn't see it coming. Surprise, surprise!

Here's how it happens: When you start to think about something that is more complex than your typical easy decision, you will get a few initial ideas on how to deal with it very quickly. The more complex the situation, the fewer ideas you will have for how to deal with it.

Once you have your first set of ideas, you analyze them quickly and find what seems to be the best course of action between those, and *bam*! This is where most people's thought process stops because it is where thinking sometimes becomes a little harder and a little frustrating. It is where you come out of your comfort zone, out of your autopilot, and consciously think about what is going on. It's where you begin to consider the

157

pieces of the puzzle that you *don't* know.

I've found that typically, the best decisions come after the third round of ideas. Are you the type of person who doesn't often make it to the second round?

In discussions with other people, you can quickly tell which ones consistently stop at the first round of ideas. They are quick to jump to erroneous conclusions and may even become defensive of those conclusions when challenged.

A person who is really looking for the best outcome doesn't get married to any idea, they are willing to entertain any relevant idea, even when they disagree with it. If their conclusion is logically defeated, they immediately adopt the winning conclusion without remorse and without feeling defeated. They welcome any improvement on their worldview.

Making it across that first plateau and thinking a little beyond what just came easily to your mind will turn you into a much better decision-maker. But really, it's when you don't stop there and persist until the third wave of ideas to come in, and then sometimes even hold out for the fourth and beyond, that you can really call yourself a good decision-maker. The key is in knowing that the second, third, and fourth waves will come, even though you can't imagine them during your first few ideas. You just need to give your mind time to get there and have faith that they will come.

It's incredibly important to be aware that one minute spent thinking about something is better than five seconds; five minutes is better than one minute, and half an hour is better than five minutes. It is impossible—seriously, *impossible*—for you to think in one minute what you can think in five. Your first few ideas will almost never be the best ones because subsequent ideas will build on the previous ones; you will take more things into account.

Obviously, don't spend two hours thinking about what color shirt you will wear today. But maybe do spend two hours thinking about what makes you feel fulfilled. Do spend one workday researching that company that wants you to invest your life savings in them. Do spend one week choosing the best company to handle your renovation project. Do spend one month figuring out your next life objective. Do spend one year deciding if your partner is the right one for you... You get the point. Little impact, little time; big impact, big time.

Take this with a pinch of salt. If you are an expert in a field, you are likely to make very good decisions in that field much faster than other people. It is not a mandate that the fourth idea will be better than the second one. You may have already found the best idea on your second wave, but you would never know unless you walk the distance and make it to the fourth wave.

Decisions

- Do you think you have mostly made good decisions or bad decisions in your life?

- Think of a bad decision you have made. Do you see what caused you to make the bad decision? If it wasn't totally your fault, can you see the part that was your fault?

- Think of a good decision you have made. Can you identify what key knowledge or intuition you had in reaching that good decision?

- Think of something that happened in your life due to a lack of decision from you or because of living on autopilot. Could you have made a difference by making a conscious decision?

Decisions are a central component of what you consider your identity—what makes you, you. Through decisions, you can modify your values, beliefs, customs, and even your emotions.

If you make decisions in a way that is inconsistent with your values or your beliefs, you create a void in you that is very difficult to fill. You lie to yourself and confuse yourself about who you are.

If you are not happy with your values, beliefs, or emotions, make the decision to change them. Only you have the final say on what you consider important.

If you are not happy with your decisions, then improve them by sticking to your beliefs and values. This will help you stop making crappy decisions. Few things are as important as being true to yourself.

An uncomfortable truth is that comfort turns us into weak decision-makers. The lack of severe repercussions allows us to make a decision today and change our minds three days later. That's why it's hard to follow a diet, stop your vices, or do what is right, even when you know what it is.

Think about it, making a decision that would have immediate, severe consequences on your life if ignored is much less likely to be disregarded. It takes much more effort to do the harder thing when we can easily do the easier thing, and not immediately feel any negative consequences.

On the other hand, to never go back on any decision would be unrealistic. You should expect to default on some of your decisions sometimes and strive to stick to them better next time. In this case, the concept of being on and off-track is very visible in our decisions, where those who get back on track faster and are more consistent with their values live better lives.

161

Actions

Actions are how you impact the world; they are where you come out of your internal process of feeling, thinking, and deciding, and do something that has the ability to impact everyone else. This means that your actions are the most reliable piece of information anyone other than yourself has in order to understand you.

Always remember that actions speak volumes. It doesn't matter what you say if you constantly act in a way that is inconsistent with your words. You may be able to trick people with them at first, but anyone who gets to know you over a period of time will know if you walk your talk.

Your actions are also where the behaviors you have decided to emulate become clearly visible.

One of the great benefits of becoming aware of what your life is really about is the realization that you may have bad experiences in life that cause you sorrow, but you can still find fulfillment through your thoughts, decisions, and actions.

- Think of some actions you took that you were not forced to take and brought negative results. What could you have done better?

- Think of some actions you took that brought positive results. Why did you take those actions?

- Think of how you want others to perceive you. Do you want to be seen as the responsible person, the smart person, the YOLO person, the careless person, the indifferent person, the fun person, the helpful person, a mix of those, or something else?

- Think of how those who know you may perceive you based on your actions and behaviors up until now. Is it in line with the perception you want others to have of you? Should you do anything differently?

Now that you have at least a glimpse of your life video, you can see that sometimes you have been on track, and other times not so much. This can even be split into different areas. For example, you may be on track financially because you are making the money you want, but not physically because you haven't been working out or eating healthy.

In your day-to-day life, you will take countless actions. These are what others will see. They won't see the difficulties you went through, the thoughts you had, or the emotions you felt, and it would be unrealistic for you to expect others to see these things.

You must come to terms with this: perception is 100% reality to the receiver. Through introspection, you take control of the image you project to the world; you build your own person according to what you consider important. Without self-examination, you relinquish control over yourself and live your life on autopilot; you let life happen to you, rather than you happening to life. You accept defeat by not caring whether you make a positive or negative impact on others. Refusing to accept the importance of perception in our society today, is the equivalent of an immature child sticking their fingers in their ears and screaming, "Lalalalalalala!"

"The unexamined life is not worth living." (Socrates)

Your Life Map

Have you had objectives, things you've wanted to accomplish, a life you've been wanting to live, a way you've been wanting to feel? Of course you have. What have you been doing to get there?

Imagine you have a big map in your hands right now. Do it! Your arms are wide open as you hold it and look at it. It's the map of your life.

You are at the center of it, and tomorrow, you will have moved in a certain direction. You have the power to decide today in which direction to move. If you move in the direction of your dreams today, when you open your map tomorrow and look at it, you will be a little closer to your dream. If you don't move in the direction of your dreams, you won't have made any progress—you may even have moved further away if you went in the opposite direction.

Depending on how far that dream is, you may want to consider some pit-stops on the way or break down your dream destination into smaller pieces so that you can see the progress more easily and plan better.

Nothing beats good old pen and paper to plan the route to your dreams. To get started, all you need to do is write down the very first step you need to take that will get you closer to your dream and give it a date. Once you have it, commit to taking the actions required to execute that step by the chosen date. Don't bother with planning all the steps; just plan the first one, as small as it can be; the first step is the hardest one. Once you have completed it, plan the next one right away.

As you successfully take your first three steps, when you think about what you are going to do next to move in the direction of your dreams, it's important to not lie to yourself by always taking the path of least resistance—doing what is easy and not what is needed. You may try to convince yourself that watching learning videos to improve yourself is the best use of your time, when in reality, you already have everything you need to take the next step that actually takes you closer to where you want to go.

Think of ways to validate your progression. How are you further along today than yesterday? It's very easy to lie to yourself that you are moving toward your destination when you are just stuck in a loop, going in circles. Moving in the right direction is not the same as just moving in any direction.

I hope you are paying attention because here comes one of the biggest time-savers of all time. Ready?

- What do salespeople do? They sell. They don't spend 80% of their time building a website and devising strategies. They knock on doors and make cold calls.

- What do teachers do? They teach. They don't spend 90% of their time perfecting the lesson they never gave.

- What do people who are fit do? They work out, even when they don't feel like it.

- What do people who change their lives do? They actually take steps to change their life. They don't sit around all day complaining about how bad the world is to them.

- What do innovators do? They innovate. They bring to life new things, not imagine how they will bring to life new things that they haven't thought of yet.

Whatever it is you say you want to do, are you actually doing it? You are either doing it or you are not; no ifs or buts. Stop choosing the easy, comfy path to oblivion and start taking conscious, relevant action in your life. Get on your way to your dreams and stop just looking at them from the distance, waiting for them to happen magically.

Time will unforgivingly and unapologetically judge whether you have made progress toward your destination or not, whether you like it or not. If you are not true to your own self, then as time goes by, uncomfortable feelings of self-deception will set in. Not dealing with them will make you dig a deeper hole into your own self-deception.

If you are honest with yourself about your shortcomings and accept that you are a human who is not always on track, you open your mind to not letting the past hold you back and to using it purely for information. It gives you permission to turn the page and decide *today* in which direction you want to move, regardless of what happened in the past. It allows you to break the behavioral patterns that keep blocking you from moving forward.

Now you know this, you are free to open your map at any time and see clearly if you have been moving toward your destination of choice or not, if you have decided to take the highway there or the scenic route.

Every life journey is unique. Some find their purpose early on, others later. Some reach their wildest dreams early on, others later.

Are you 20, 30, 40, 50, or 60? Don't let the past drag you down and don't let the future be fully unknown. You know what you will do every single day, regardless of what that day brings. Use this knowledge wisely, and live a forever improving and fulfilling life.

> *"The best thing about the future is that it comes one day at a time."*
> *(Abraham Lincoln)*

Closing Thoughts

Now that you have taken the time to read this book, I have one final question for you. Go back in your mind to when you started reading, to the moment when I asked you about your definition of life. Did you have one? If so, has this book helped you to develop or improve it? Did it confirm the definition you already had? Have you accepted the one I proposed?

The understanding of what a human life is and what it takes to live a fulfilled life can become a piece of knowledge that you possess in your mind and that no one can take away from you. You can tailor it, change it, perfect it—do whatever you want with it—as long as you truly feel it in your bones, that it is as close to the truth as you can get, and just as important, that it is practical!

If I have added value to your understanding of life through this book, or at least made you think about it constructively, consider bringing up the topic of what life is about in your next gathering with friends, colleagues, or family. You will see how surprised people become with the question and how difficult it will be for them to collect their thoughts if they attempt to really give you a coherent answer. This will prove to you how uncommon it is for someone to have clarity on what life really is about for themselves and how myopic most answers are.

When asking the question, the key is to keep our definition of life present in your mind. It's about experiences, thoughts, emotions, decisions, and actions, because those are the things we will do every single day of our lives and we are incapable of not doing them. Life is about doing those things over and over again.

As they are giving you their answers, look for common ground on the ideas that seem similar to our definition and seek agreement on those. For example, someone saying life is about being at peace with themselves is likely to agree with the thoughts and emotions part of our definition.

You can then expand to ask about the pieces of our definition they seem to have left out, and about anything they mentioned that seems incorrect. For example, if their answer was that life is about success, money, or happiness, they would appear to mostly focus on the experiences part, and to give little consideration to the other parts of our definition. You can ask clarifying questions about those.

Once you make it through the 'what life is about' part, if you have the stamina, you can set out to explore fulfillment. How does their definition of life allow them to live a fulfilled life?

Finally, if you enjoyed this book and consider it important, help others find it by leaving a review where you purchased it; short or elaborate, I read them all!

"We are what we repeatedly do. Excellence, then, is not an act, but a habit." (Aristotle)

Note on
Pillars of Self-Actualization

Thanks to the studies of a great psychologist named Abraham Harold Maslow, today, we have a more profound understanding of what our needs are and how they influence our lives.

In his publication, *A Theory of Human Motivation*, he made an invaluable gift to humanity, known as Maslow's Hierarchy of Needs. Self-Actualization is the culmination of this hierarchy; it represents the stage at which humans can achieve their highest potential.

In short, as humans, we all have the same four basic needs: Physiological/Survival, Safety, Love and Belonging, and Self-Esteem. It's only after these four needs are satisfied to a certain extent, that your mind finds itself available to dedicate some mental space to the higher need known as Self-Actualization. This is where you come out of your bubble and make your greatest contributions to the world!

I hold the firm belief that the more space your mind can dedicate to Self-Actualization, the better a person you become; and the more people who get there, the better the world we live in.

This is the vision that motivates me to write the Pillars of Self-Actualization. This series aims to accelerate a person's growth so that they can satisfy the first four levels of the hierarchy as much as possible and in their own unique way. I am convinced that once the four basic needs are sufficiently satisfied, there is only one direction in which to look next, and that is toward Self-Actualization.

To build these pillars, it's important to get to the practical truths of life and to communicate them in ways people can relate to. In pursuit of these, I am interested in continuously improving my understanding of the world by incorporating new perspectives into my analyses.

If you have a perspective to share or a principle you would like to discuss, reach out—it may well find its way to my next book!

"We all have everything we need within us to create our fullest potential." (Abraham Maslow)

Meet the Author

Ernesto became infatuated with Maslow's Hierarchy of Needs early on, then found a passion for philosophy through Plato's dialogues, his preference leaning towards epistemology.

He has devoted tens of thousands of hours to the study of life's challenges from a diverse range of perspectives. As a result of this process, he developed the uncanny ability to tackle some of life's most elusive questions with practical and universal answers designed to withstand the test of time.

His origins took him from Havana to Montreal, where he graduated from the John Molson School of Business to South Florida, where he lives with his wife and son.

His passions and multicultural background come together in his writings to create a pragmatic lens that sharply pierces through the veil of old, engrained, misconceptions, and provides clarity in an era of cloudy misinformation.

Using first principles thinking, he steps away from specialized jargon and endless theoretical discussions, into relatable everyday life experiences and common language, ultimately leading to intuitive and actionable knowledge.

He aims to equip his readers with wisdom that empowers them to live ever-more fulfilling lives.

You can connect with him at https://www.erleyva.com